Contents

To the teacher

Intentions

Parallel Poems is a teaching anthology of paired poems for GCSE/Standard Grade courses. Its 15 units are designed to support students in:

✧ reading poetry as a worthwhile and imaginatively engaging activity, fully integrated with the other elements of GCSE English and English Literature.

✧ responding personally to poems by working on them as much as possible in interactive contexts and in task-centred ways.

✧ becoming familiar with a very wide range of poetic forms and styles, drawn from both contemporary and pre-twentieth-century sources.

✧ comparing/contrasting the subject-matter and style of poems, to assist the comparative study of literature now prescribed for all GCSE courses.

✧ acquiring the skills necessary to face with confidence GCSE poetry examinations, including 'unseens'.

Unit design

Each unit is built around two 'core' poems which are comparable in theme and/or form and style. Most units incorporate the following common features:

✧ Preliminary activities for small groups and pairs, to establish an appropriate context for students before they read the poems.

✧ A wide variety of post-reading tasks, both spoken and written, to help students develop their own understanding of what they have read.

✧ End-of-unit written assignments of a formal kind, differentiated to cater for the needs of the whole ability range.

✧ Instructions in using terminology suitable for writing about poetry in GCSE coursework and terminal examinations.

Activities within each unit, and throughout the book as a whole, have been planned to develop students' reading and response skills in a progressive way.

Parallel

Poems

A *comparative* *approach for* *Key Stage* 4

MIKE ROYSTON

Stanley Thornes (Publishers) Ltd

First published in 1996 by:
Stanley Thornes (Publishers) Ltd
Ellenborough House
Wellington Street
CHELTENHAM GL50 1YW
England

96 97 98 99 00 / 10 9 8 7 6 5 4 3 2 1

A catalogue record for this book is available from the British Library.

ISBN 0–7487–2574–1

Acknowledgements

The author would like to thank GCSE students at Finham Park School, Coventry, and at The Billericay School, Essex, for helping to develop material used in this book.

The author and publishers wish to thank the following for permission to use copyright material:

James Berry for 'In-a Brixtan Markit' from *Chain of Days*, Oxford University Press, 1985 ● Rosica Colin Ltd on behalf of the author for Alan Brownjohn, 'We Are Going To See The Rabbit', 1983. Copyright © Alan Brownjohn 1983 ● J M Dent Ltd on behalf of the author for R. S. Thomas, 'Depopulation of the Hills' from *Collected Poems 1945-1990* ● Faber and Faber Ltd for Seamus Heaney, 'Mid-Term Break' from *Death of a Naturalist* ● HarperCollins Publishers Ltd for Mick Gowar, 'First Love' from *So Far So Good*, Collins ● David Higham Associates on behalf of the author for Elizabeth Jennings, 'Absence' from *Collected Poems*, Carcanet ● Macmillan General Books for Thomas Hardy, 'Neutral Tones' from *The Complete Poems* ● John Murray (Publishers) Ltd for John Betjeman, 'In Westminster Abbey' from *Collected Poems*, 1958 ● Polygon for Liz Lochhead, 'Men Talk' from *True Confessions and New Cliches* ● Random House UK Ltd on behalf of the Estate of Robert Frost for 'The Need of Being Versed in Country Things' from *The Poetry of Robert Frost*, edited by Edward Connery Latham, Jonathan Cape, 1971 ● Rogers, Coleridge & White Ltd on behalf of the author for Edward Lucie-Smith, 'The Lesson' from *A Tropical Childhood and Other Poems*, Oxford University Press, 1961. Copyright © Edward Lucie-Smith 1961 ● George Sassoon for Siegfried Sassoon, 'Glory of Women' from *Collected Poems*, Faber and Faber ● Virago Press for Grace Nichols, 'The Fat Black Woman Goes Shopping' from *The Fat Black Woman Poems* ● Gwen Watkins for Vernon Watkins, 'The Collier' from *The Ballad of the Mari Lwyd*, Faber and Faber, 1947 and in *Selected Poems 1930-1966*, Faber and Faber, and in *The Collected Poems of Vernon Watkins*, Golgonooza Press, 1986. Copyright © Gwen Watkins ● G. M. Wilson for Raymond Wilson, 'This Letter's To Say' and 'Old Johnny Armstrong' ● The Andrew Young Estate for Andrew Young, 'Hard Frost' from *Poetical Works*, Secker and Warburg, 1985.

Also the following for permission to reproduce photographs and illustrations:

Andes Press Agency pages 1, 28 (centre), 93 (right) ● Corbis pages 44, 86 (right) ● Eye Ubiquitous pages 20, 86 (left), 92, 93 (left), 110 (left) ● Chris Fairclough Colour Library pages 18, 28 (left), 118 (left) ● Geoff Howard page 57 (right) ● Hulton Deutsch Collection pages 37 (right), 48, 52, 101 (left), 126 (right) ● Images Colour Library pages 11 (left), 67 (right) ● Imperial War Museum page 76 (right) ● Peter Kent pages 57 (left), 67 (left) ● London Planetarium page 94 ● Mansell Collection pages 101 (right), 110 (right), 118 (right) ● Mary Evans Picture Library pages 21, 22 ● Rex Features pages 28 (right), 76 (left), 126 (left) ● Simon Warner pages 11 (right), 37 (left).

Every effort has been made to trace all the copyright holders, but if any have been inadvertently overlooked the publishers will be pleased to make the necessary arrangement at the first opportunity.

Typeset by Tech-Set Ltd, Gateshead, Tyne and Wear.
Printed and bound in Great Britain at Scotprint Ltd, Musselburgh, Scotland.

The price of progress?

This Letter's To Say — RAYMOND WILSON

'We Are Going To See The Rabbit...' — ALAN BROWNJOHN

Every year we build more and more estates, houses and flats to accommodate more and more people. Extra roads and motorways are needed to cope with the growing amount of traffic.

Both poems in this unit ask:

✧ what happens when governments and local councils use up 'green land' for new roads and houses?

✧ is it 'progress' or a human nightmare?

✧ where will it all end?

Pre-reading activity on both poems

ACTIVITY 1 — *The Marshdown Bypass*

In a small group, read the information below. It is the basis for a role-play which you will later act out.

> You live in the small Cotswold village of Marshdown. It is a pretty, 'olde-worlde' place with a population of under 1,000. It has become extremely popular as a local beauty spot and attracts many visitors.
>
> At the moment, the main A95 road runs right through the centre of Marshdown. It carries heavy traffic, including juggernaut lorries and HGVs, between two large industrial towns.
>
> It has been proposed that a bypass should be built, diverting through-traffic from the village. The bypass will provide a detour across land presently used for farming, 3 miles to the west of the village.
>
> The local district council has called a meeting to give village people the chance to put forward their views on this proposal. A heated argument has been going on in Marshdown ever since the bypass plans were published.
>
> The following people are among those present at the meeting:
>
> **Mrs Ash**   Landlady of Marshdown's only pub, The Feathers, which dates back to Elizabethan times. With her husband, she has run the pub for 25 years. Her son and his wife own the largest shop in the village: a general store and post office. Mrs Ash is **against the bypass** because:
>
> ✧ she is likely to lose business at The Feathers if traffic is diverted. She and her husband have built up a successful bed-and-breakfast trade.
>
> ✧ her son and his wife will suffer by losing custom at the general store.
>
> **Miss Brown**   Secretary of the Village Residents' Association. She lives in an original eighteenth-century house (a listed building) in the main street. Her elderly mother is disabled and confined to a wheelchair. Miss Brown is **in favour of the bypass** because:
>
> ✧ she believes that traffic pollution in Marshdown is a serious health-hazard. Lead and carbon monoxide levels are well above the official danger limit.

✧ she feels that Marshdown has been turned into a 'black spot': it is a dying community since many villagers have moved elsewhere, driven out by the noise and danger caused by excess traffic.

Mr Clark   The farmer who owns much of the land through which the proposed bypass will run. His farm is on 30 acres of some of the best crop-rearing and fruit-growing land in the Cotswolds and he is Chairman of the Cotswold Conservation Trust. Mr Clark is **against the bypass** because:

✧ his farm will be destroyed and the compensation payment would be a mere fraction of what the land is worth.

✧ as Chairman of the Cotswold Conservation Trust, he opposes the threat to local vegetation and wildlife: the ecological balance of the area will be upset by building the bypass.

Mr Dent   The headteacher of the village school. He has lived in Marshdown all his life and traced its history right back to the Domesday Book. He is particularly interested in local vegetation and wild flowers, some of which are unique to this area. Mr Dent is **in favour of the bypass** because:

✧ he is worried that HGVs driving through Marshdown are weakening the foundations of historic buildings.

✧ he is aware of the danger of accidents posed by heavy traffic. School children and the elderly are especially at risk.

Role-play the village meeting.

Each member of your group should play the part of one of the village residents listed above. As long as you stay in role, you are free to say what you like.

Take about ten minutes to prepare. The points above are meant to start off your role-play. Use your own ideas as the discussion gets under way. Make sure that everyone is given a fair chance to state their case.

Finally, hold a class discussion in which you consider 'the price of progress' in your own area. How much new building has taken place recently? Has the natural environment been affected by it? What are the views of local residents?

The poems Read both poems to yourself, slowly, one after the other.

As you read, try to work out what each poet is saying about the way new building affects people and wildlife.

This Letter's To Say

Dear Sir or Madam,
This letter's to say
Your property
Stands bang in the way
Of Progress, and
Will be knocked down
On March the third
At half-past one.

There is no appeal,
Since the National Need
Depends on more
And still more Speed,
And this, in turn,
Dear Sir or Madam,
Depends on half England
Being tar-macadam.
(But your house will –
We are pleased to say –
Be the fastest lane
Of the Motorway.)

Meanwhile the Borough
Corporation
Offer you new
Accommodation
Three miles away
On the thirteenth floor
(Flat Number Q
6824).

But please take note,
The Council regret:
No dog, cat, bird
Or other pet;
No noise permitted,
No singing in the bath
(For permits to drink
Or smoke or laugh
Apply on Form
Z 327);
No children admitted
Aged under eleven;
No hawkers, tramps
Or roof-top lunches;
No opening doors
To Bible-punchers.

Failure to pay
Your rent, when due,
Will lead to our
Evicting you.
The Council demand
That you consent
To the terms above
When you pay your rent.

Meanwhile we hope
You will feel free
To consult us
Should there prove to be
The slightest case
Of difficulty.

With kind regards,
Yours faithfully…

RAYMOND WILSON

4

'We Are Going To See The Rabbit...'

We are going to see the rabbit,
We are going to see the rabbit.
Which rabbit, people say?
Which rabbit, ask the children?
Which rabbit?
The only rabbit,
The only rabbit in England,
Sitting behind a barbed-wire fence
Under the floodlights, neon lights,
Sodium lights,
Nibbling grass
On the only patch of grass
In England, in England
(Except the grass by the hoardings
Which doesn't count).
We are going to see the rabbit
And we must be there on time.

First we shall go by escalator,
Then we shall go by underground,
And then we shall go by motorway
And then by helicopterway,
And the last ten yards we shall have to go
On foot.

And now we are going
All the way to see the rabbit,
We are nearly there,
We are longing to see it,
And so is the crowd
Which is here in thousands
With mounted policemen
And big loudspeakers
And bands and banners,
And everyone has come a long way.

But soon we shall see it
Sitting and nibbling
The blades of grass
On the only patch of grass
In – but something has gone wrong!
Why is everyone so angry,
Why is everyone jostling
And slanging and complaining?

The rabbit has gone,
Yes, the rabbit has gone.
He has actually burrowed down into the earth
And made himself a warren, under the earth,
Despite all these people.
And what shall we do?
What *can* we do?

It is all a pity, you must be disappointed,
Go home and do something else for today,
Go home again, go home for today.
For you cannot hear the rabbit, under the earth,
Remarking rather sadly to himself, by himself,
As he rests in his warren, under the earth:
'It won't be long, they are bound to come,
They are bound to come and find me, even here.'

ALAN BROWNJOHN

Did you know...

✧ At the moment (1996) the population of England is about 53 million. By the year 2050, it will have risen by 20 per cent.

✧ In 2050 more than three-quarters of British people will be living in towns and cities.

✧ Every day over 100,000 vehicles use the M25 motorway.

✧ Today there are 60,000 km of major roads in England. This figure is set to double over the next fifty years.

Post-reading activities on both poems

ACTIVITY 2   *A note for the future*

With a partner, take turns to read both poems aloud. You can each read the whole of one poem. Alternatively, you may find it more effective to divide the poems up into sections and read these in turn.

Both poets are imagining what life might be like in the not-too-distant future. They have based their ideas on what is happening in this country *now*. Working together, make a 'note chart' for each poem to show all the things in them that are different from everyday life today.

Do it like this, using one sheet of paper per poem:

This Letter's To Say

1   *People forced out of their homes to make way for new roads, without the right of protest*

2   *Half the country covered by roads ('tar-macadam')*

'We Are Going To See The Rabbit...'

1   *Only one rabbit left in the whole of England*

2   *People do almost no walking at all*

Try to list at least five points on your note chart for each poem. You will probably find many more, especially about '"We Are Going To See the Rabbit..."'

When you have finished, join up with another pair. Compare your ideas. Be prepared to explain why you have written what you have by referring back to the exact words used in the poems.

Getting further inside the poems

With a partner, decide who is **A** and who is **B**. Act out two situations based on the poems. Stay in character throughout, looking back at each poem to work out what you are going to say.

Situation 1 on 'This Letter's To Say'

A is a householder who has received the letter which makes up the poem. B is the Council Official who has sent it.

A has taken up the offer to 'feel free to consult us [if there is a] difficulty'. B has arranged a face-to-face meeting at the Council Offices. The scene begins with A being shown into B's office.

Use the details in the poem to decide:

✧ how many things will **A** have to complain about? What will they be?

✧ what reasons will **B** give for the decisions the Council has taken, as set out in the letter? How will he or she explain the need to evict **A**?

✧ what tone of voice will **A** use? What tone is right for **B**?

Situation 2 on 'We Are Going To See The Rabbit...'

B is an enthusiastic member of the public who has travelled a long way to see the rabbit. A is a policeman/woman who has to explain why the rabbit has gone to ground. The scene begins with B saying: 'Well, I'm not going home till I've seen it.'

Use the details in the poem to decide:

✧ how many things will **B** have to complain about? What will they be?

✧ how will **A** explain why the rabbit is not able to be seen? What will he or she advise **B** to do instead?

✧ what tone of voice will **B** use? What tone is right for **A**?

<u>Activity 4</u>   *Comparing and judging*

On your own:

a Write an account of the view of 'progress' and the future presented in these poems. Describe any differences, as well as similarities, you can find between them.

b Give your opinion about which of the poets is better at getting his ideas across. Some of the things to ask yourself before deciding are:

❖ why does Raymond Wilson choose to write his poem in the form and style of a letter? Is this an effective device?

❖ why does Alan Brownjohn choose to write most of his poem from the viewpoint of someone 'going to see the rabbit'? Why does he *change* the viewpoint in the last stanza? Is this effective?

❖ do the rhymes in 'This Letter's To Say' help to convey the poem's message more strongly – or do they add to the difficulty of understanding it?

❖ does the way in which the lines are set out in 'We Are Going To See The Rabbit' help or hinder your understanding of it?

❖ do you find either poem too 'far-fetched' to take seriously?

c Look closely at the photograph on page 1 and the illustration on page 6. Write about them briefly, giving your views on:

❖ the feelings each image arouses in you.

❖ which image you feel is better suited to the title of this unit, 'The price of progress?'.

End-of-unit further writing suggestions

On your own:

a Re-read the 'Did you know…' panel on page 6. Imagine you are living in the year 2050.

Write *either*

✧ an account of a typical day in your life, bringing out the problems you face, *or*

✧ a story based on the over-crowded state of the country, showing how people try to cope.

b Imagine that you have received the letter in Raymond Wilson's poem.

Write a letter in reply to the Borough Corporation. Draw on the role-play you did in Activity 3 for some of your ideas about what to write.

You need to decide:

✧ whether to accept the demand that you should move to 'new accommodation' in view of the 'National Need'.

✧ how you are going to explain your decision to move or not to move.

✧ whether the style and tone of your letter should be angry and aggressive or polite and restrained.

c Put forward some of your own ideas for preventing Britain from getting into the state described in the poems in this unit.

What you write about is up to you. You may like to consider, among other things:

✧ how we can prevent the unchecked growth of traffic (and therefore of roads).

✧ how the countryside and wildlife can be protected.

✧ how the nation's growing population can be accommodated without swallowing up more and more open land.

She says, he says

Men Are...   THE RAVING BEAUTIES

Men Talk   LIZ LOCHHEAD

The poems in this unit take a critical look at the two sexes.
The first one, written from a female viewpoint, is very
sarcastic about men. The second criticises the ways in which
women are supposed, according to *some* men, to behave.

Both poems are in the form of raps. They are meant to be
heard aloud rather than read silently. A lot of your work in
this unit involves performing the poems in order to bring
them to life.

Pre-reading activity on both poems

ACTIVITY 1   *Gender attitudes*

Form a small group. If your class is a mixed one, make up single-sex groups. Four people per group is the ideal number.

Get a large sheet of paper and write on the top of it:

Annoying things members of the opposite sex do at parties

Discuss what you are going to put under this heading. Anyone in the group can write down a point, as long as other people agree with it.

Here are a few ideas to get you started. They are taken from a conversation on this subject by students of your own age.

Girls talking about boys

'They show off all the time… you know like "I'm really macho"… "I'm dead fanciable". Yuk!'

'They talk really loud about… oh, I don't know – football, fighting, bikes, how much they spend on CDs. And they belch a lot, on purpose.'

'They're so immature, aren't they?'

Boys talking about girls

'If you ask them to dance, or have a drink or something, they start to giggle… they do! …and they whisper to their mates behind their hand. Embarrassing!'

'They keep on going to the loo every five minutes… but they always take a friend with them. Have you noticed that?'

'They're really immature, aren't they?'

Try to come up with about ten points.

When your group has finished, take turns to read out to the rest of the class what you have written, point by point. Make sure that everyone in the group makes a contribution.

The poem   Read the poem below to yourself. Being a rap, it has a strong rhythm. As you read, try to hear this rhythm inside your head.

Remember that the poem is being unpleasant about men. Imagine reading it aloud in a highly sarcastic tone.

Men Are...

men are strong
men are tough
men are surly, men are rough
men have mates
men drink beer
men are brave and don't show fear
men slap backs
men sing songs
men are men and men are strong
men don't touch
men aren't drips
men shake hands with vice-like grips.

men like fighting
men like cars
men like shouting with men in bars
men like football
and now and then
men like men like men like men
no they don't
men beat up queers
men live with their mums for years and years
men have beards
and hairy chests
men walk through blizzards in string vests.

men can embrace
and bare their soul
but only if they've scored a goal
men leap tall buildings
men are tough
men don't know when they've had enough
men drive fast cars with wide wheels
men like fur-lined steering-wheels
men have muscles
men have sweat
men haven't learned to grow up yet.

men climb mountains
in the snow
men don't cook and men don't sew
men are bosses
men are chums
men build office blocks and slums
men make bombs
men make wars
men are stupid, men are bores
men ignore
what women see
and call our story **his**tory.

THE RAVING BEAUTIES

Post-reading activities on 'Men Are...'

ACTIVITY 2   *Rapping (1)*

In the same group as you were in for Activity 1, rap out a group performance of 'Men Are...'

Plan this carefully and rehearse several times before you perform.

Planning your performance

✧ Everyone needs their own photocopy of the poem.

✧ Decide which lines each person will speak. Underline or highlight your 'bits'. (The only rule is that no one should perform the whole of one stanza.)

✧ Discuss which words you are each going to emphasise.

Rehearsing and performing

✧ Practise getting the **rhythm** and the **speed** absolutely right. Should the speed change or stay the same throughout?

✧ The most important part of your performance is the **tone of voice** you use, to match up with the meaning of the lines.

When the groups are ready, each performs in turn. If possible, put the performances on tape and play them back in a later lesson.

ACTIVITY 3   *Poetry on display*

Form a small group. 'Men Are...' contains more than forty statements about men. Using a large sheet of paper or card, make a collage to illustrate in picture form at least twelve of these. Then put it on display.

Do it like this:

✧ Look through magazines and newspapers for pictures which match any of the lines in the poem (for example, 'men are brave and don't show fear'... 'men drive fast cars with wide wheels'). Cut these out.

✧ When you have collected as many pictures as you can find, spread them out on your paper or card. Agree on the arrangement that looks best. Then stick them down.

✧ Write out the relevant lines from 'Men Are...' to match the pictures. These become the captions which complete your collage.

The poem   Read the poem below to yourself. Try to 'hear' it in your head.

Men Talk

Women
Rabbit rabbit rabbit women
Tattle and titter
Women prattle
Women waffle and witter

Men Talk. Men Talk.

Women into Girl Talk
About Women's Trouble
Trivia 'n' Small Talk
They yap and they babble

Men Talk. Men Talk.

Women yatter
Women chatter
Women chew the fat, women spill the beans
Women aint been takin'
The oh-so Good Advice in them
Women's Magazines.

A Man Likes A Good Listener.

Oh yeah
I like A Woman
Who likes me enough
Not to nitpick
Not to nag and
Not to interrupt 'cause I call that treason
A woman with the Good Grace
To be struck dumb
By me Sweet Reason. Yes –
A Man Likes A Good Listener

A Real
Man
Likes a Real Good Listener

Women yap yap yap
Verbal Diarrhoea is a Female Disease
Woman she spread rumours round she
Like Philadelphia Cream Cheese.

Oh
Bossy Women Gossip
Girlish Women Giggle
Women natter, women nag
Women niggle niggle niggle
Men Talk.

Men
Think First, Speak Later
Men Talk.

LIZ LOCHHEAD

Post-reading activities on 'Men Talk'

ACTIVITY 4   *Rapping (2)*

With a partner, get a photocopy of 'Men Talk'. Decide carefully how you are going to divide the poem up between you for performance. Plan and rehearse, following the advice in Activity 2.

When you are ready, give your performance.

| ACTIVITY 5 | *Sounds the same* |

With the same partner as you had for Activity 4, look back over 'Men Talk'. In the course of the poem, Liz Lochhead uses many words describing the way women are supposed to speak which sound the same as their meaning. This is known as **onomatopoeia**.

Between you, write down a list of these onomatopoeic words. You should be able to find about fifteen. You may need to look up some of their meanings in the dictionary. When you have finished your list, read the words aloud in turn. Go through the whole list twice, putting as much expression as possible into the way you pronounce them.

Post-reading activity on both poems

| ACTIVITY 6 | *Style and structure* |

Each poem is set out, or structured, in a deliberate way to get across its meaning clearly. The meaning is also emphasised by certain aspects of style, particularly **sound** and **tone**.

Talk as a whole class about the style and structure of these poems by considering the questions which follow.

Men Are…

✦ There are four stanzas in the poem. Would it matter if they came in a different order? Give a reason for what you decide.

✦ Do you think the **rhythm** and **pace** (i.e. the reading speed) should be the same all the way through, or should the rhythm change at certain points?

✦ The 'voice' of the poem is a woman's. Where do you think the **tone** of this voice is at its most

        mocking   humorous   bitter   serious?

✦ Do you think this poem is meant as an entertaining, light-hearted 'send up' of men, or is it a hard-hitting condemnation of the male sex which we are asked to take seriously? Give reasons for your opinion.

Men Talk

✧ There are eleven stanzas in this poem, three of which are only one line long. Why do you think Liz Lochhead has divided up 'Men Talk' in this way?

✧ Re-read the first stanza. Where does the poet use

repetition of words?

rhyme?

alliteration (repetition of the same letter sound)?

Give your ideas about why Liz Lochhead uses these devices.

Look at the rest of the poem. How many other examples of repetition, rhyme and alliteration are there? What effects are gained by these at the particular points in the poem where they occur?

✧ The 'voice' of the poem is a man's. Where do you think the tone of this voice is at its most

       scornful   vain   patronising   self-righteous?

Judging by the tone as well as what 'he' says, what picture of the man who is speaking do you have in your mind?

✧ Why do you think Liz Lochhead, a woman, wrote this poem? Do you think it is more, or less, effective than 'Men Are…'?

End-of-unit further writing suggestions

On your own:

a Write to either Liz Lochhead or The Raving Beauties saying what you think is fair or unfair in the way they portray the two sexes.

Use your own experience, including what you have read or seen on TV or film, to support the points you make.

b Write a story based on sexist attitudes and/or behaviour. Bring out the *consequences* of sexism in the way you present and shape your story.

You can draw on your own experience in deciding what to write, or you can make your story entirely fictional.

c The teenagers quoted in Activity 1 claimed that, at your age, members of the opposite sex are often 'immature'. Do you agree?

Write about this subject in whichever way you think suits it best. You might choose, for example:

✧ a playscript.

✧ a poem.

✧ a letter to a teenage magazine.

✧ a story.

✧ an article for a newspaper.

d The media, especially newspapers and TV, are sometimes accused of 'sex stereotyping'. Evidence of this tends to be drawn from:

✧ advertisements.

✧ coverage of sport.

✧ coverage of the royal family.

✧ characters in sitcoms.

✧ comedians' jokes.

Using actual examples, say whether you agree that the media give a distorted view of one or both of the sexes. If so, what should be done to correct it?

Winter reflections

Snowday   KAREN MILLER

Hard Frost   ANDREW YOUNG

The poems in this unit are about harsh weather. They describe the effect on two different landscapes of winter suddenly arriving with its armoury of sleet, frost, snow and ice.

Both poems are 'picture poems'. They are mainly concerned with how things look. Consequently, the poets make a lot of use of visual **images** – a word that simply means 'pictures painted in words'.

The use of images often involves making comparisons to show as clearly as possible what something looks like. In working through this unit, you will become familiar with three terms that describe a writer's use of comparisons: **simile**, **metaphor** and **personification**.

Pre-reading activity on both poems

ACTIVITY 1 *Reading pictures*

With a partner, decide who is **A** and who is **B**.

Spend a few minutes looking at the picture which corresponds to your letter.

Describe it as if talking to someone who is blind. Your other partner acts as the unsighted listener. Your job is to make him or her 'see' it as clearly as possible.

Refer to the image as a whole, but concentrate particularly on describing the details numbered ① to ⑥.

A goes first.

Picture A

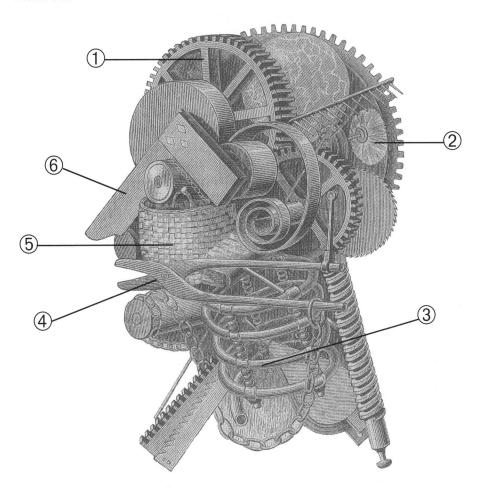

Picture B

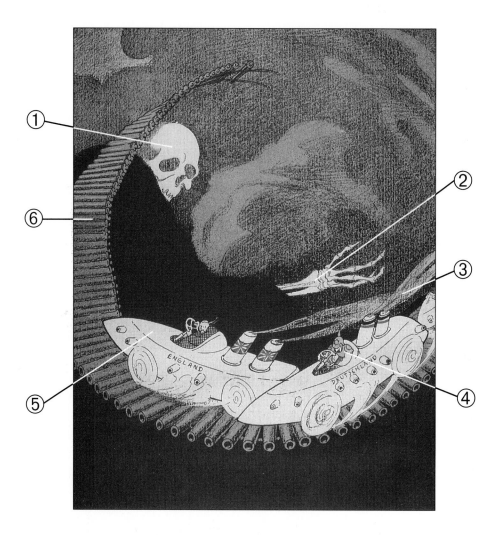

Join up with another pair. Tell your opposite number what you said to make your partner visualise the picture. Did you make up any comparisons to help you?

With your opposite number, or on your own, write an unrhymed poem of between six and ten lines describing the main visual details in your picture. Give it a title which sums up its overall atmosphere or mood. Set out the lines in a way that you feel suits the image.

The poem   Read the poem on this page to yourself, twice. It was written by a student of your age.

Snowday

December sky hangs low. It's like a bruise
That spreads across white skin, not really black
Just yet, but threatening to hurt. The air
Squeezes your lungs. Steam-kettle breath escapes,
Rising in curls, in light-grey streamers. Car   5
Headlights carve their yellow tracks through fog,
The drivers, hunched as moles, groping for home.
By morning, snow will, like a landslide, fall.

It does. My window's blind with metalled frost,
Its eyeball full of ferns. The fence wears gloves.   10
Across the lawn, a quilted bedspread furls,
Pock-marked by birds on stilts. The pond's been trapped.
Our drive is polished glass, where dad – dressed like
An eskimo – slithers and rocks the car.
Downstairs, the radio drones. Mum calls: 15
'Don't bother getting up. They've closed the school!'
I snuggle, like a squirrel, back to bed.

                                                        KAREN MILLER

Post-reading activity on 'Snowday'

ACTIVITY 2   *Spot the likeness*

In a small group, read the information below.

A **simile** is a comparison in which something is directly said to be like something else. For example, 'the wind cut like a knife' or 'the wind was as sharp as a razor'. Usually you can find similes by looking for the words 'like' or 'as'.

A **metaphor** is a comparison in which one thing is compared with another, but the comparison is not directly stated by using 'like' or 'as'. For example, 'the rain bucketed down'.

Personification is a form of comparison in which something non-human and ordinary is described as though it is a human or an animal. For example, 'the darkening sky frowned down on the city' or 'the jagged teeth of the wind bit into my skin'.

Each of you should have a large sheet of paper.

Read carefully through each line of the poem by Karen Miller. She has used quite a number of comparisons to describe the way things *look*, and sometimes to give an impression of how things *feel*.

Pick out all the **similes**, **metaphors** and uses of **personification** you can find. Discuss them briefly by asking each other:

✧ What, exactly, is being compared with what?

✧ Does the comparison give a really clear picture?

Then, on your sheet of paper, make a 'comparison chart' on which you list the similes, metaphors and examples of personification you have identified.

Do it like this:

Line number	The two things being compared	Simile/metaphor/ personification
1 and 2	The December sky and a bruise on the skin	Simile
4	Breath rising in the winter air and steam coming out of a kettle	Metaphor

10	The bedroom window and an eye	Metaphor
17	The writer of the poem and a squirrel	Simile

When you have finished, take the two comparisons which you think are the most effective in the poem and the two you think are least effective. Tell each other the reasons for your opinion.

Then join up with another group. Compare your charts with theirs. Does either group have examples which the other missed?

The poem Read the poem on this page to yourself, twice. The first time through, concentrate only on getting the general idea of what it describes. The second time through, read more slowly: keep stopping, and try to fix in your mind as clearly as possible the pictures it paints.

You may need to refer to the glossary of unfamiliar words at the end of the poem.

Hard Frost

Frost called to water 'Halt!'
And crusted the moist snow with sparkling salt;
Brooks, their own bridges, stop,
And icicles in long stalactites drop,
And **tench** in water-holes   5
Lurk under gluey glass like fish in bowls.

In the hard-rutted lane
At every footstep breaks a brittle **pane**,
And tinkling trees ice-bound,
Changed into weeping willows, sweep the ground;   10
Dead boughs take root in ponds
And ferns on windows shoot their ghostly **fronds**.

But **vainly** the fierce frost
Interns poor fish, ranks trees in an armed host,
Hangs daggers from **house-eaves**   15
And on the windows ferny ambush weaves;
In the long war grown warmer
The sun will strike him dead and strip his armour.

ANDREW YOUNG

tench: freshwater fish
pane: i.e. pane of glass
fronds: fern-leaves
vainly: in vain, without success
Interns: imprisons, keeps captive
house-eaves: the overhanging edges of roofs

Post-reading activities on 'Hard Frost'

ACTIVITY 3   *Explaining metaphor and personification*

With a partner, take a photocopy of the poem and two different coloured pens or pencils.

Read the poem aloud, dividing it up between you in any way you wish.

On your photocopy, draw brackets round the phrase 'like fish in bowls' (line 6). This is the only **simile** in the poem.

Then, with one of your coloured pens, underline all the **metaphors** you can find. For example, 'Brooks, their own bridges' (line 3). When you have finished this, underline in a different colour each example of **personification** you can spot. For example, 'Frost called to water "Halt!"' (line 1).

Each get a large sheet of paper. Make two 'comment charts' on which you explain what you think is the point of each metaphor and personification Andrew Young uses in his poem. In the right-hand column of each chart, say how effective you feel these are by writing **Good**, **All right** or **Poor**.

Do it like this:

Metaphors		
Line number	My explanation	Opinion
3	Brooks are like bridges because when they freeze over you can walk across the water on the ice	?

Uses of personification		
Line number	My explanation	Opinion
1	The frost is like a soldier on guard stopping the water from moving by calling 'Halt!'	?

ACTIVITY 4   *A pattern of comparisons*

Form a small group. Sometimes poets use metaphor and personification in such a way that it makes a 'pattern' of comparisons throughout an entire poem. This is true of 'Hard Frost'.

Appoint a note taker from your group. At the top of a sheet of paper, he or she writes 'The Long War' – a phrase Andrew Young uses on line 17.

Everyone should now look through the poem again, finding as many references as possible to war in general, battles, fighting and weapons.

You will need to look hard: some of these references are quite deeply buried. As you find them, your note taker should write them down.

When you have finished, discuss the idea of 'the long war' in 'Hard Frost'. What is Andrew Young's purpose in creating a pattern of language, especially comparisons, connected with warfare?

Appoint someone from your group (not the note taker) to act as a spokesperson, and share your conclusions with the rest of the class.

Post-reading activity on both poems

ACTIVITY 5   *Written commentary*

On your own, choose *either* 'Snowday' *or* 'Hard Frost'.

Drawing on the work you have done throughout this unit, write a commentary on the meaning (or 'theme') of your chosen poem. Pay particular attention to the poet's use of comparisons as you explain what the poem is about.

To conclude your commentary, say whether the poet's use of comparisons – simile, metaphor and personification – makes what he or she has written more effective. Quote particular examples to back up your opinion.

4 *Out of place*

The Fat Black Woman Goes Shopping
GRACE NICHOLS

In-a Brixtan Markit
JAMES BERRY

No More Boomerang
KATH WALKER

In this unit, the poems are about people who feel like aliens in the place where they live. Grace Nichols, who comes from Guyana, and James Berry, a Jamaican, are West Indians writing about their life in London. Kath Walker puts herself in the place of an Australian aboriginal whose community is being destroyed by the white man.

These poems are not written in Standard English. The poets' 'voices' in this unit are the real voices of people who feel, or who are made to feel, displaced.

Pre-reading activity on all poems

<u>ACTIVITY 1</u>   *Changing places?*

In a small group, read the information below which gives details on which to base a role-play. It is a real-life situation but the names have been changed.

The Harris family faces a tough problem. John Harris, 41, is a manager employed by a company with branches throughout Europe. Due to falling sales, the company is closing down its British base where John has worked for sixteen years. He has been offered a choice between redundancy or an equivalent managerial job at the company's Italian base in Genoa.

The family has two teenage children. Jason, 17, is halfway through his A levels at sixth-form college. Sally, 14, is in Year 9 at a private school with an excellent reputation. Both children are happy, settled and doing well in their studies.

Sue Harris, 40, has returned to her career as a NHS staff nurse after a break to bring up her children.

The Harrises live in a four-bedroomed detached house. They bought it for £110,000 in the 1980s when house prices were high. As a result, they have a large 20-year mortgage.

John has already tried for other management posts locally, without any success. He has been advised that, at his age, it will be 'virtually impossible' to find a similar job with another company in this country.

The Harrises now have less than a month to decide what to do. They are a close-knit family and none of them wants to be split.

Role-play the discussion where the family decides whether or not to move to Italy. Each person in your group acts as one member of the Harris family.

You can say what you wish as long as it is based on the given information. Add further details as you see fit. For example:

❖ perhaps Sally has an Italian pen-friend and knows the basics of the language.

❖ Sue is likely to have found out if she can use her nursing skills in Italy.

In the course of discussion, each member of the family will talk about the changes, for good or bad, involved in moving abroad.

The poems Read the following poems to yourself, one after the other.

The Fat Black Woman Goes Shopping

Shopping in London winter
is a real drag for the fat black woman
going from store to store
in search of accommodating clothes
and de weather so cold

Look at the frozen thin mannequins
fixing her with grin
and de pretty face salesgals
exchanging slimming glances
thinking she don't notice

Lord it's aggravating

Nothing soft and bright and billowing
to flow like breezy sunlight
when she walking

The fat black woman curses in Swahili/Yoruba
and nation language under her breathing
all this journeying and journeying

The fat black woman could only conclude
that when it come to fashion
the choice is lean

Nothing much beyond size 14

GRACE NICHOLS

In-a Brixtan Markit

I walk in-a Brixtan markit,
believin I a respectable man,
you know. An wha happn?

Policeman come straight up
and search mi bag!
Man – straight to mi.
Like them did a-wait fi mi.
Come search mi bag, man.

Fi mi bag!
An wha them si in deh?
Two piece a yam, a dasheen,
a han a banana, a piece a pork
an mi lates Bob Marley.

Man all a suddn I feel
mi head nah fi mi. This yah now
is when man kill somody, nah!

'Tony', I sey, 'hol on. Hol on,
Tony. Dohn shove. Dohn shove.
Dohn move neidda fis, tongue
nor emotion. Battn down, Tony.
Battn down.' An, man, Tony win.

JAMES BERRY

Post-reading activities on both poems

ACTIVITY 2 — *Accent and dialect*

With a partner, look very carefully at each poem in turn. They are both written in a form of West Indian dialect.

Without any help from your teacher, try to sort out what Grace Nichols and James Berry are saying in their poems.

When you have understood the poems as well as you are able, join up with another pair and compare your interpretations.

ACTIVITY 3 — *Dialect and style*

Form a small group. The questions below ask you to look closely at the style in which each poem is written. After talking through your answers, put them down on paper.

The Fat Black Woman Goes Shopping

✧ The most obvious meaning of 'a real drag' (stanza 1) is 'a bore'. What further meanings could Grace Nichols have in mind?

✧ Why do you think the Fat Black Woman sees the mannequins in the dress shops as being 'frozen thin' (stanza 2)?

✧ The salesgirls are said to be giving each other 'slimming glances' (stanza 2). What does this metaphor mean?

✧ The Fat Black Woman chooses the simile 'like breezy sunlight' (stanza 4) to describe the kind of clothes she would like to find. Why might she have picked this particular comparison?

✧ Why do you think the Fat Black Woman repeats herself at the end of stanza 5?

✧ There is more than one reason why the Fat Black Woman calls the choice of clothes in the shops 'lean' (stanza 6). Explain both the meanings of this word, and say how it sums up what the poem is really about.

In-a Brixtan Markit

✧ James Berry writes this poem as if Tony is telling his story to a friend – perhaps sitting by him or her, speaking face-to-face. Point out three aspects of the poem's style which help to give this effect.

✧ The word 'fi' is used three times in the poem. On each occasion it has a different meaning. Say what the three meanings are.

✧ Why do you think Tony takes up three whole lines of the poem to list all the items in his bag?

✧ In the last few lines of the poem, Tony is speaking to himself. The seven sentences he uses are all very short. Why do you think this is?

✧ The poem ends: 'An, man, Tony win.' What does he mean by this? Do you agree with him?

ACTIVITY 4   *The poems in performance*

Work with a partner. The best way to show your understanding of poems is to perform them, reading aloud with the right kind of expression, tone, volume and rhythm.

Prepare to perform both poems by discussing the following things.

✧ What mood is the Fat Black Woman in? Does her mood stay the same all through, or does it change at any point? How are you going to get her mood across in your performance?

✧ At what speed would it be best to read Grace Nichol's poem?

✧ There are many single words in the Fat Black Woman poem which need to sound long and drawn-out. Decide which they are.

✧ Tony is not angry all the way through James Berry's poem. He has other feelings as well. How will you get these across?

✧ Tony's character is important to your reading. Discuss it.

When you feel well prepared, each of you should give a performance of both poems. Take it in turns. If possible, record this on tape.

The poem　Read the poem on this page to yourself twice – once to get used to the language and once to start taking in what the aboriginal speaker is telling us about the changes that have transformed his life.

Australian aboriginals led a traditional native life until many of them were recruited as workers for mines and factories – the owners of which were white men. As a result, the aboriginals supposedly enjoyed a higher standard of living.

No More Boomerang

No more boomerang
No more spear;
Now all civilized –
Colour bar and beer.

No more **corroboree**,
Gay dance and din.
Now we got movies,
And pay to go in.

No more sharing
What the hunter brings.
Now we work for money,
Then pay it back for things.

Now we track bosses
To catch a few bob,
Now we go walkabout
On bus to the job.

Bunyip he finish,
Now got instead
White fella Bunyip,
Call him Red.

Abstract picture now –
What they coming at?
Cripes, in our caves we
Did better than that.

Black hunted wallaby,
White hunt dollar;
White fella witch-doctor
Wear dog-collar.

No more message-stick;
Lubras and lads.
Got television now,
Mostly ads.

One time naked,
Who never knew shame;
Now we put clothes on
To hide whatsaname.

No more **gunya**,
Now bungalow,
Paid by higher purchase
In twenty year or so.

Lay down the stone axe,
Take up the steel,
And work like a nigger
For a white man meal.

No more firesticks
That made the whites scoff.
Now all electric,
And no better off.

Lay down the **woomera**,
Lay down the **waddy**.
Now we got atom-bomb,
End *every*body.

KATH WALKER

corroboree: an aboriginal festival
Bunyip: a make-believe monster
Lubras: women
gunya: hut
woomera, *waddy*: native weapons

Post-reading activities on 'No More Boomerang'

ACTIVITY 5   *Discovery reading*

With a partner, decide who is **A** and who is **B**. Read 'No More Boomerang' aloud in the following way:

✦ For each stanza, **A** reads the first two lines, **B** the last two.

✦ Because he or she is describing what the aboriginal has lost, **A** should sound sad, angry and hurt.

✦ Because he or she is describing what the aboriginal has now got but does not want, **B** should sound bitter, scornful and sarcastic.

Rehearse your reading once, then perform the poem together, bringing out the strong feelings it contains by the way you speak.

Now discuss what you have learned about the differences between the aboriginal's old and new way of life. You should be able to come up with at least ten differences.

ACTIVITY 6   *In the hot seat*

Form a group of four. Two people will take on the role of white factory owners who believe the aboriginals are now better off in every way. Two people play the part of aboriginals who believe the exact opposite. All four of you must stay in character.

The factory owners are in the 'hot seat'. The aboriginals question them hard about the supposed benefits of their new way of life. For example:

✦ We used to enjoy our **own** entertainments and festivals. Now all we've got is TV and the movies. Do you call that being 'civilized'? What good is it doing us?

✦ Instead of our native witch-doctors we now have **your** Christianity. Why can't we have our witch-doctors back?

The aboriginals should put at least six points to the factory owners, based on the information in the poem.

When both pairs are fully prepared, hold your hot seat session.

$\mathcal{P}$*ost-reading activities on all poems*

ACTIVITY 7   *Drawing the poems together*

Talk as a whole class about your response to the poems in this unit by considering the questions which follow.

a   What difference would it make if the poems were written

✧ in Standard English?

✧ in the third person rather than the first person?

b   How does each poem use humour to make its point? Quote examples. Do you find the humour effective?

c   Which of the poems makes you feel most sympathetic to the person speaking in it? Why?

d   The National Curriculum for English (Key Stage 4/GCSE) states:

✧ 'pupils should read texts from other cultures and traditions.'

✧ 'pupils should learn to appreciate both the need for Standard English and occasions when non-standard forms are required for effect.'

Do you agree? Have the poems in this unit affected your opinion?

ACTIVITY 8   *Personal response*

On your own, give your personal response to at least two of the poems in this unit by writing on one of the titles below.

✧ In what ways do the writers of these poems show the people they describe to be 'out of place'?

✧ What do the poems make you feel about the displaced people in them? How does the way in which they are written help to arouse these feelings in you?

End-of-unit further writing suggestions

On your own:

a Write a true or imagined account of someone going away from home, either by themselves or with others, perhaps for the first time.

Your writing could describe, for example:

❖ moving house.

❖ moving to another part of the country.

❖ going abroad on holiday.

❖ going to live overseas.

❖ any other experience of 'uprooting'.

b Imagine that you are a member of the Harris family in Activity 1. You *did* move to Italy.

Write a sequence of diary entries covering the first six months of your stay (or longer, if you wish). Describe the changes you had to cope with, how you felt about your new surroundings, and how successfully you managed to adjust.

c Many people go through feelings of being out of place in the course of their normal, everyday lives. These feelings can arise from what seems like a trivial cause when it's looked back on: at the time, however, it feels devastating.

If you have had similar feelings, write about them in the form of either a story or a poem.

d Write about the experiences of a newly arrived immigrant to this country trying to adapt to a new way of life.

What difficulties do they have fitting in? How do they attempt to overcome them? Do they succeed?

Your writing can be based on your own experience, on what you have heard from friends, or it can be entirely imaginary. The form in which you write is up to you.

Coming to terms

Mid-Term Break   SEAMUS HEANEY

The Lesson   EDWARD LUCIE-SMITH

The poems in this unit are about young people facing up to the death of a relative. In one case it is a younger brother who dies; in the other case, a father.

When their relatives died, the poets were still boys. Each was away at boarding-school when he heard the news. These poems describe the feelings they had at the time.

In the course of this unit, you will be looking closely at the particular choices of **language** poets make: why *that* word, phrase or term rather than another?

Pre-reading activity on both poems

<u>ACTIVITY 1</u>   *Every word in place*

Form a small group. The purpose of this activity is to help you prepare for working on 'Mid-Term Break' and 'The Lesson'.

Read the poem below to yourself, twice. The first time through, concentrate on getting an impression of the kind of life Old Johnny Armstrong lives. On your second reading, form some idea of the poet's attitude towards him. Ten words have been omitted from the poem.

Old Johnny Armstrong

Old Johnny Armstrong's eighty or more
And he ① like a question-mark
Over two ② sticks as he shuffles and picks
His slow way to Benwell Park.

He's lived in Benwell his whole life long
And remembers how street-lights came,
And how once on a time they laid a tram-line,
Then years later dug up the same!

Now he's got to take a lift to his flat,
Up where the ③ winds blow
Round a Council Block that rears like a rock
From ④ of swirled traffic below.

Old Johnny Armstrong lives out his life
In his ⑤ on the seventeenth floor,
And it's seldom a neighbour will do him a favour
Or anyone knock at his door.

With his poor hands ⑥ with rheumatism
And his poor back ⑦ in pain,
Why, day after day, should he ⑧ his slow way
To Benwell Park yet again? –

O the wind in park trees is the self-same wind
That first blew on a village child
When life freshly ⑨ in a green, lost world
And his ⑩ limbs ran wild.

RAYMOND WILSON

Look together at the ten numbered gaps in the poem. From each gap one word has been omitted. Select the word you think fits best into each space.

Make your choices from the table below:

Space	Choice			
1	leans	bends	humps	stoops
2	old	gnarled	wooden	thin
3	tall	cold	fierce	cruel
4	fumes	swarms	seas	miles
5	home	nest	cell	flat
6	knotted	riddled	twisted	useless
7	buckled	doubled	huddled	hurting
8	limp	make	slouch	pick
9	uncurled	revived	emerged	unfurled
10	youthful	straight	childish	proud

Your choices must be thoughtful and reasoned. For example:

✧ Consider the four possibilities for the first space. Does 'bends' give a clearer picture of the old man than 'humps'? Would someone who stoops look 'like a question-mark'? Is there any difference in meaning between 'leans' and 'stoops'? If so, which word applies better to the posture of an old person using two walking-sticks?

✧ Ask yourself which word best fits the mood and feeling of the whole poem.

If you disagree with others in your group, back up your choice by explaining in detail why you have made it.

Everyone should keep his or her own list of choices. You can then compare them with those the poet actually made. The full version of the poem is printed on the next page. Do not look at it until you have completed this activity. If you find differences, there is every reason for preferring your own words, as long as you can justify them to other readers.

Old Johnny Armstrong

Old Johnny Armstrong's eighty or more
And he humps like a question-mark
Over two gnarled sticks as he shuffles and picks
His slow way to Benwell Park.

He's lived in Benwell his whole life long
And remembers how street-lights came,
And how once on a time they laid a tram-line,
Then years later dug up the same!

Now he's got to take a lift to his flat,
Up where the tall winds blow
Round a Council Block that rears like a rock
From seas of swirled traffic below.

Old Johnny Armstrong lives out his life
In his cell on the seventeenth floor,
And it's seldom a neighbour will do him a favour
Or anyone knock at his door.

With his poor hands knotted with rheumatism
And his poor back doubled in pain,
Why, day after day, should he pick his slow way
To Benwell Park yet again? –

O the wind in park trees is the self-same wind
That first blew on a village child
When life freshly unfurled in a green, lost world
And his straight limbs ran wild.

RAYMOND WILSON

40

The poem   Read the poem on this page to yourself, twice – once to clarify the story it tells and once to note the feelings Seamus Heaney has about his young brother's death.

Check the meanings of any words you may find new to you. Several are given at the foot of the page.

Mid-Term Break

I sat all morning in the college sick bay
Counting bells **knelling** classes to a close.
At two o'clock our neighbours drove me home.

In the porch I met my father crying –
He had always taken funerals in his stride –
And Big Jim Evans saying it was a hard blow.

The baby cooed and laughed and rocked the pram
When I came in, and I was embarrassed
By old men standing up to shake my hand

And tell me they were 'sorry for my trouble'.
Whispers informed strangers I was the eldest,
Away at school, as my mother held my hand

In hers and coughed out angry tearless sighs.
At ten o'clock the ambulance arrived
With the corpse, **stanched** and bandaged by the nurses.

Next morning I went up into the room. Snowdrops
And candles soothed the bedside; I saw him
For the first time in six weeks. Paler now,

Wearing a poppy bruise on his left **temple**,
He lay in the **four foot box** as in his cot.
No gaudy scars, the bumper knocked him clear.

A four foot box, a foot for every year.

SEAMUS HEANEY

knelling: ringing or tolling, as at a funeral
stanched: the flow of blood has been stopped
temple: side of the head
four foot box: i.e. the young boy's coffin

$\mathcal{P}$ost-reading activity on '$\mathcal{M}$id-$\mathcal{T}$erm $\mathcal{B}$reak'

ACTIVITY 2   *Charting the poet's feelings*

Form a small group. Seamus Heaney is clearly upset by his brother's death, but his feelings change depending on the circumstances he is in during the poem.

Show these changes of feeling by making a 'mood graph'. You will each need a sheet of graph paper.

It is important that you think hard about, and discuss, how upset Heaney is at each stage in the poem before you plot your graph. For example, is he more upset by his father crying than he is by his mother crying? Is he less upset by the sight of his dead brother than by waiting for the ambulance to arrive?

Do it like this:

✧ Decide where in the poem Heaney is *most* upset. On your graph, make a small 'x' in pencil to show in which stanza this occurs.

✧ Then decide where in the poem Heaney is *least* upset. Plot this on your graph with another pencilled 'x'.

✧ Now look carefully at the rest of the poem and plot the other changes in Heaney's feelings, showing the different degrees of sadness he experiences.

The framework of your graph will look like this:

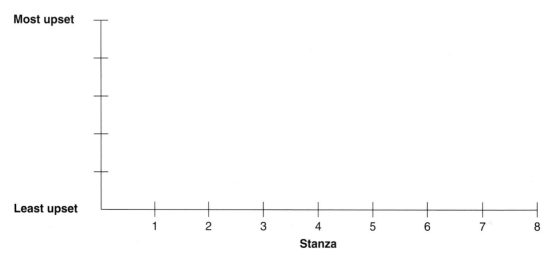

When you have plotted all the changes in Heaney's feelings, join up your crosses. You will then have a description, in diagram form, of how his feelings fluctuate in the course of the poem.

The poem Read the poem below once to yourself. There is a glossary at the end to explain some less familiar words.

The Lesson

'Your father's gone,' my bald headmaster said.
His shiny **dome** and brown tobacco jar
Splintered at once in tears. It wasn't grief.
I cried for knowledge which was bitterer
Than any grief. For there and then I knew
That grief has uses – that a father dead
Could **bind** the bully's fist a week or two;
And then I cried for shame, then for relief.

I was a month past ten when I learned this:
I still remember how the noise was stilled
In school-assembly when my grief **came in**.
Some goldfish in a bowl quietly **sculled**
Around their shining prison on its shelf.
They were **indifferent**. All the other eyes
Were turned towards me. Somewhere in myself
Pride like a goldfish flashed a sudden fin.

EDWARD LUCIE-SMITH

dome: head
bind: hold back, stop
came in: was made known to everyone
sculled: propelled themselves, swam
indifferent: unconcerned, without feelings

Post-reading activity on 'The Lesson'

ACTIVITY 3   *Interviews in role*

With a partner, read the poem aloud, taking one stanza each. In the first stanza, Lucie-Smith has been called in to the headmaster's study to be told in private of his father's death. In the second stanza, the news is announced in assembly to the whole school.

Decide who is **A** and who is **B**. You are both going to put yourself in the poet's shoes. **A** will pretend to be Lucie-Smith in stanza 1. **B** will do the same for stanza 2.

After looking again at stanza 1, **B** interviews **A** (i.e. Lucie-Smith) about his feelings, asking such questions as:

✦ What did you feel like when you were summoned to the headmaster's office?

✦ Why did you burst into tears when he first told you the news about your father?

Try to ask and answer five questions. **A** must answer in role, using the facts given in stanza 1, but adding anything else which is consistent with what we are told.

Now look again at stanza 2. **A** interviews **B** (i.e. Lucie-Smith) about his feelings, asking such questions as:

✦ How did you feel when everyone in assembly went quiet as your father's death was announced?

✦ Why did your mind fix itself on those goldfish in their bowl?

Try to ask and answer five questions, in the same way that **A** did earlier.

Post-reading activities on both poems

Close-up on language

Form a small group. Good poets do not write anything without good reason. They draft and re-draft until every word and phrase says exactly what they want it to.

Look back to 'Mid-Term Break'. Discuss why you think Seamus Heaney chose the words and phrases highlighted below. Don't worry if your ideas differ from other people's: poets often pack more than one meaning into what they write.

✧ Counting bells **knelling** classes to a close (stanza 1).

✧ And Big Jim Evans saying **it was a hard blow** (stanza 2).

✧ In hers and **coughed** out **angry tearless sighs** (stanza 5).

✧ **Wearing a poppy bruise** on his left temple (stanza 7).

✧ He lay in the four foot box **as in his cot** (stanza 7).

Now look at the words and phrases highlighted below, quoted from 'The Lesson'. Discuss them in the same way.

✧ 'Your father's **gone**,' my bald headmaster said (stanza 1).

✧ **Splintered** at once in tears. It wasn't grief (stanza 1).

✧ Around their **shining prison** on its shelf (stanza 2).

✧ Pride **like a goldfish** flashed a sudden fin (stanza 2).

Consider briefly the importance to the whole poem of:

✧ the goldfish in their 'prison' in 'The Lesson'.

✧ the last line of 'Mid-Term Break', standing on its own.

ACTIVITY 5   *In comparison*

As a whole class, talk about the similarities and differences between these poems. Use the questions below to focus your discussion.

Subject-matter

a Both poets feel deeply about the deaths they describe. In what ways are their feelings alike, and in what ways do they differ?

b By the end of each poem, what do you think the boys learned about

✧ death?

✧ themselves?

Setting and atmosphere

c In 'Mid-Term Break', there are three settings: the college sick bay, the porch and living-room of the family home, and the dead brother's bedroom. What is the atmosphere of each setting? In which setting do you think Seamus Heaney comes to terms with his brother's death most fully?

d In 'The Lesson', there are two settings: the headmaster's study and the school assembly-hall. How and why do these different settings influence Edward Lucie-Smith's feelings about his father? In which setting do you think he feels the impact of his father's death most strongly?

Viewpoint

e We see both deaths through youthful eyes. What impressions have you formed of the personality of each boy? Which of the two strikes you as being the less mature? Why?

Style and structure

f How well-suited is the title of each poem to what it describes and to the way it is written?

g Imagine that each poet had written in sentences and paragraphs rather than in lines and stanzas. Would it have made any difference to the effect of the writing on you?

ACTIVITY 6   *Written comparison*

On your own, draw on the work you have done throughout this unit, particularly the class discussion, to write a comparative commentary on 'Mid-Term Break' and 'The Lesson'. Use this title:

Compare and contrast the feelings of Heaney and Lucie-Smith about the death of a relative. Quote from the text to make clear the similarities and differences you find.

Compare the ways in which the poems are written. Say which poet you think is the more successful in getting his feelings across, and why.

End-of-unit further writing suggestions

On your own:

a Both poems mention other people who were involved with the death being described or with the news about it.

Write a conversation in playscript form between one or more of the following:

✧ Heaney's parents.

✧ Heaney and his mother.

✧ Big Jim Evans and the 'old men' in 'Mid-Term Break'.

✧ Several pupils in Lucie-Smith's class, including a bully.

✧ Lucie-Smith's headmaster and another teacher at the school.

b Seamus Heaney and Edward Lucie-Smith were educated at boarding-school.

What are the arguments for and against boarding-schools? Write a discussion essay putting forward your own views. Whatever your opinion, try to consider the other side of the argument.

c The poems in this unit describe young people's feelings towards their parents. In common with most people in their early or mid-teens, these feelings are mixed.

Write a private letter to one or both of your parents. What you write depends on the present state of your relationship with them, and the reasons for it. Whatever your feelings are, express them in an honest, forthright way.

You are not required to show what you write to your teacher or to anyone else in school. If you choose to show the letter to your parents, you may like to ask them to write a reply.

6

Trapped underground

The Gresford Disaster   ANONYMOUS

The Collier   VERNON WATKINS

In this unit, the poems are about the serious dangers and
hardships of coal-mining. The first describes a pit accident in
Wales in the 1930s, when working conditions were far more
hazardous than they are today. The last is Vernon Watkins'
autobiographical poem about being 'trapped' by his mining
background into working down the local pit.

Each poem is a **ballad**: that is, a poem which tells a story in a
particular form and style. Your work in this unit will introduce
you to the special characteristics of ballads, and show how
'story poems' can be used in quite different ways.

The poem   Read the poem on this page aloud with a partner. There are eight stanzas. Read them turn by turn.

The Gresford Disaster

You've heard of the Gresford disaster,
The terrible price that was paid;
Two hundred and forty-two colliers were lost
And three men of a rescue brigade.

It occurred in the month of September;
At three in the morning that pit
Was wracked by a violent explosion
In **the Dennis** where dust lay so thick.

The **gas** in the Dennis deep section
Was packed like snow in a drift,
And many a man had to leave the coal-face
Before he had worked out his shift.

A fortnight before the explosion
To **the shot-firer**, Tomlinson cried:
'If you fire that shot we'll be all blown to hell!'
And no one can say that he lied.

The fireman's reports they are missing,
The records of forty-two days,
The colliery manager had them destroyed
To cover his criminal ways.

Down there in the dark they are lying,
They died for nine shillings a day;
They've worked out their shift and it's now they must lie
In the darkness until Judgement Day.

The Lord Mayor of London's collecting
To help both the children and wives.
The owners have sent some white lilies
To pay for the colliers' lives.

Farewell our dear wives and our children,
Farewell our dear comrades as well.
Don't send your sons in the dark dreary mine,
They'll be damned like the sinners in Hell.

ANONYMOUS

the Dennis: the name given to the deepest section of the Gresford mine
gas: methane, a hydrocarbon gas, which often builds up in mines and which
    can be lethal because it explodes so fiercely
the shot-firer: in the 1930s, coal was mined by dynamiting the coal-face – a
    shot was fired to blow up the dynamite

Background facts

The story told in this poem is a true one. The explosion which destroyed the Gresford coal mine near Wrexham occurred at 3 a.m. on Saturday, 23 September 1934. About 400 men were working the night-shift. The methane gas in the Dennis section of the pit ignited. It caused a violent explosion, followed by such a fierce fire that rescue teams could not get near the men. It was more than six months before anyone was able to go down the pit. The official death-toll was 264.

In the 1930s, before Britain's coal mines were nationalised, each pit was privately owned. The owners employed colliery managers to supervise the work. There was no Miners' Union. The men often worked in highly dangerous conditions and were paid very low wages.

Post-reading activities on 'The Gresford Disaster'

ACTIVITY 1   *A case history*

Work with a partner. You have been commissioned by the editor of a forthcoming book entitled *Disasters of the Twentieth Century* to prepare an account of the tragedy at Gresford. Your first task is to make detailed notes, based on your understanding of the poem.

Work through the poem stanza by stanza. Note down all the information you can find under the following headings:

✧ Exactly what happened, and why?

✧ Could the accident have been avoided?

✧ Who was to blame?

Make sure that you cover every detail.

Sometimes you will need to 'read between the lines'. For example, in stanza 2 we are told: 'In the Dennis where dust lay so thick'. How might this have contributed to the explosion that took place?

You should each make your own notes as you work through the poem. When they are complete, join up with another pair. Add to what you have written if other people have spotted things you have missed. Do not yet turn your notes into a fully written account for the book.

ACTIVITY 2   *The ballad form (1)*

Form a small group. The poem you have been working on is a ballad. The aim of this activity is to learn something more about the form and style in which ballads are written.

To do so, first read another version of the Gresford mine accident.

Black Death

Dai was a Gresford man,
a miner, like his dad before him
who'd died, aged 50, with two lungfuls of dust.
(Black Lung, they called it.)

Dai married, had kids, drank
when he could afford it
(not much beer on nine bob a day).
At weekends, played rugger.

Dai worked the Friday night shift
to be free for Saturday's game
(big match, see, against Wrexham).
He never kicked off.

Dai worked the Dennis, dust-choked
bitch of a seam. Coughed on the gas
(remembering his dad coughing to death).
One night it lit up.

Dai was a Gresford man,
a miner, like his sons became,
who died, aged 40, with charred stumps for legs.
(Black Death, they called it.)

MIKE ROYSTON

Compare these two poem versions of the same event. Think and talk about the following things:

✧ In what ways is 'The Gresford Disaster' more like a short story than 'Black Death'?

✧ Why are the stanzas in 'The Gresford Disaster' like eight consecutive paragraphs in a short story?

✧ Which version would you find easier to use if you were making a film about what happened at Gresford? Why?

✧ Why is 'Black Death' less like a song than 'The Gresford Disaster'?

✧ Imagine reading these two versions to someone who was quite young. In which of them is the language easier to follow?

✧ Look at the rhyme pattern in 'The Gresford Disaster'. Does each stanza rhyme in the same way?

✧ 'The Gresford Disaster' is anonymous. It was not written to be published. Why do you think it has managed to survive to the present day?

Each take a sheet of paper. Write a heading:

The typical qualities of a ballad

You can assume that 'The Gresford Disaster' is a typical ballad.

Draw on the discussion you have had and list all the qualities you can think of. You should be able to come up with at least six. Keep on sharing your ideas.

When you have finished, be prepared to contribute to a class discussion on the topic, 'What is a ballad?'

The poem   Read the poem below, first to yourself, then aloud with a partner in the same way as you read 'The Gresford Disaster'.

The Collier

When I was born on Amman hill
A dark bird crossed the sun.
Sharp on the floor the shadow fell;
I was the youngest son.

And when I went to the County School
I worked in a shaft of light.
In the wood of the desk I cut my name:
Dai for Dynamite.

The **tall black hills** my brothers stood;
Their lessons all were done.
From the door of the school when I ran out
They frowned to watch me run.

The slow grey bells they rung a chime
Surly with grief or age.
Clever or clumsy, lad or lout,
All would look for a wage.

I learnt the valley flowers' names
And the rough bark knew my knees.
I brought home trout from the river
And spotted eggs from the trees.

A coloured coat I was given to wear
Where the lights of the rough land shone.
Still jealous of my favour
The tall black hills looked on.

They dipped my coat in the blood of a **kid**
And they cast me down a pit,
And although I **crossed with** strangers
There was no way up from it.

Soon as I went from the County School
I worked in a **shaft**. Said Jim,
'You will get your chain of gold, my lad,
But not for a **likely** time.'

And one said, 'Jack was not raised up
When the wind blew out the light
Though he interpreted their dreams
And guessed their fears by night.'

And Tom, he shivered his leper's **lamp**
For the **stain** that round him grew;
And I heard mouths pray in the after-damp
When **the picks would not break through**.

They changed words there in the darkness
And still through my head they run,
And white on my limbs is the linen sheet
And gold on my neck the sun.

VERNON WATKINS

tall black hills: the tips or 'slag-heaps' overlooking the mine
Surly: unfriendly, ill-tempered
kid: boy/young goat
crossed with: met with
shaft: i.e. a shaft down the mine
likely: very long
lamp: the lamp on his miner's helmet
stain: bloodstain from a mining accident Tom has suffered
the picks would not break through: the rescuers cannot reach Tom and the
    others who are trapped in the pit by a rock-fall

Post-reading activities on 'The Collier'

ACTIVITY 3   *The use of extended metaphor*

Form a small group. 'The Collier' is a modern ballad. Like 'The Gresford Disaster', it tells a true story, but in this case a personal one. The poem is Vernon Watkins' account of part of his own life as a miner.

The meaning of the story is given greater depth by the fact that Watkins uses a much older story as a frame of reference for his own. You may already have worked out what it is, either from your knowledge of the Bible or of modern musicals.

> ### *The story of Joseph and his coat of many colours*
>
> *Jacob of Canaan had twelve sons, of whom Joseph was the youngest. From early childhood, Joseph was 'different' in that he possessed visionary powers: he could foretell the future and interpret people's*

dreams. He was always his father's favourite. As a result, his eleven brothers grew jealous and treated Joseph cruelly, not allowing him to share their pastimes.

Jacob made matters worse by favouring his youngest son to such an extent that he presented him with a multi-coloured coat. The brothers were so angered by this that they abducted Joseph and dug a pit to bury him in. After stripping off his coloured coat and tearing it to pieces, they dipped it in the blood of a kid (a young goat) that they had killed. They eventually sold Joseph into slavery via a group of passing Ishmaelites, who took him in chains to Egypt. The brothers returned home with the bloodstained coat and misled Jacob into believing that Joseph had been killed by wild beasts.

In Egypt Joseph was bought by Potiphar, an army captain, and worked as a slave in his house. Before long, he was thrown into gaol for allegedly seducing Potiphar's wife. At this point, his fortunes took a turn for the better when the Pharoah heard of Joseph's ability to interpret dreams. Having correctly told the Pharoah the meaning of his dream about the impending famine that threatened Egypt, and thus saving the Egyptians from disaster, Joseph was highly rewarded. The Pharoah promoted him to the post of steward in the royal Palace and gave him many expensive gifts, including a golden chain.

In 'The Collier', Vernon Watkins uses the Joseph story as an **extended metaphor** (that is, a sustained comparison) for his own life-story when he was forced to work down the mine. There are numerous points of connection between the two stories. Work your way through the poem and find as many as you can. Then make a 'comparison chart' to show the parallels between them.

Do it like this:

Joseph's story	The Collier's story
Jacob's youngest son	The youngest son of his family
Had eleven brothers who disliked him intensely and were jealous of him	His 'brothers' were the colliery tips which 'frowned' on him and were 'jealous of my favour'
His father gave him a multi-coloured coat	He went to secondary school and wore a uniform in school colours

Try to find up to ten points of similarity between the modern story and the biblical one.

Discuss the ways in which Vernon Watkins makes use of the Joseph story to tell us of his own feelings about being a miner in the present day.

ACTIVITY 4   *The ballad form (2)*

With a partner, look back to the written work you did during Activity 2 on the typical qualities of a ballad.

In how many ways would you say 'The Collier' demonstrates these qualities? Make a list between you.

When you have finished, join up with another pair and compare lists. Have you omitted anything which they have included?

Post-reading activity on both poems

ACTIVITY 5   *Choice of written work*

On your own, write about *either* 'The Gresford Disaster' *or* 'The Collier'.

On 'The Gresford Disaster', write in full the account you prepared in note form during Activity 1 for publication in *Disasters of the Twentieth Century*.

On 'The Collier', demonstrate how Vernon Watkins uses an extended metaphor to describe his experience of the hardships of a miner's life. Comment on the way in which he uses other elements of the ballad form to tell his own story.

Whichever choice of writing you make, try to show your knowledge of the details of the poems you have studied in this unit. If you write on 'The Collier', quote frequently from the text to back up the points you put forward.

7 *Bomb scared*

When the Bomb Drops   Rebecca Dale

In Westminster Abbey   John Betjeman

In this unit, the two poems are 'spoken' by people afraid of being the victims of bombing in wartime. Rebecca Dale's poem is set in the present, under the shadow of nuclear war. John Betjeman's poem is set in the London Blitz during the Second World War.

As you read, you will become aware of the social attitudes of the speakers which the threat of being bombed brings to the surface. This unit will help you see how the style of the poems shapes our own view of the speakers, particularly through the poets' use of **satire**.

Pre-reading activity on 'When the Bomb Drops'

ACTIVITY 1   *In the nuclear shelter*

In a small group, get a large sheet of paper and appoint a note taker.

Imagine there is a renewed and urgent threat of nuclear war. Between you, you own a nuclear shelter equipped with everything you need to survive. There is, however, a limited amount of space.

Apart from yourselves, your immediate families and a few close friends, there is room for between six and eight more people. They need not be known to you personally. What kinds of people would you choose to share your shelter on the grounds that they will be of most use to you during and after the war?

For example, what might be the arguments in favour of including the following:

✧ a doctor?

✧ a town-planner?

✧ a university professor of science?

✧ an electrician?

Brainstorm a long list of up to fifteen people, then narrow it down to between six and eight. You must be clear about your reasons for choosing the people you do, and you must, by the end of your discussion, agree with each other about who they will be.

Your note taker writes down your final list of people, along with your main reasons for choosing them.

Now join up with another group and compare lists. Listen with an open mind to the reasons for their choices. They should do the same to you. In the light of this discussion, do you wish to make any changes to your list?

Finally, share your ideas in the course of a class discussion. It could take the form of a Balloon (or Raft) debate, in which different people act out the parts of those they have decided should have a place in the shelter.

The poem Read the poem on this page to yourself, twice. On your second reading, try to picture the kind of woman who is speaking in the poem. Do you know anyone like her, or does she remind you of anyone you have seen on TV? Hear inside your head the sort of accent she would have.

When the Bomb Drops
Confessions of a nuclear shelter owner

It was quite a difficult decision really –
like a Christmas card list – well, nearly.
We sat at our Georgian card table inlaid in brass
and decided on just five from out of the mass
of people in our street (we prefer to call it an avenue)   5
to share our shelter. Those people without an inside loo
should be crossed off the list, Tom said,
because he believed they were better off dead.
I wrote that down with my gold Parker pen
and put a line through the Browns at number ten.   10

After sipping Perrier we had another think
and **deleted** the Ahmeds whose skin isn't pink;
not that we're biased and they aren't totally black,
but in such important matters one cannot be slack.
One must think of the future: breeding a new race;   15
Tom says those coloureds couldn't stand the pace.
We decided against students who call their flats 'digs',
and Communists, dustmen, those who keep pigs.
Senior citizens and social workers were crossed off our list;
our dear, dear neighbours will be dearly missed.   20

Soon we discovered to our surprise
that the only people left were the Snodgrass-**Rhys**.
They're an awfully nice family – friends of ours in fact –
so we hurried over there and made a **pact**.
Now we're all ready for the nuclear bomb…   25
Just the Snodgrass-Rhys, and me… and Tom.
Actually, we think it might be rather fun.

(In case of gate-crashers Tom's got a gun.)

REBECCA DALE

deleted: crossed off
R*hys*: pronounced 'rice'
pact: agreement

Post-reading activity on ‘When the Bomb Drops’

Character profile (1)

With a partner, decide who is **A** and who is **B**.

Read the poem aloud in the following way. There are thirteen sentences in the poem. Sentence 1, for example, runs from the start of the poem to the end of line 2; the second sentence ends in the middle of line 6. Read the thirteen sentences turn by turn, starting with **A**. Use a 'posh' accent – the more extreme and exaggerated you can make this, the better. Do two readings.

Then get a large sheet of plain paper. On it, make a 'character gram' to describe the personality of the woman who is speaking.

Do it like this:

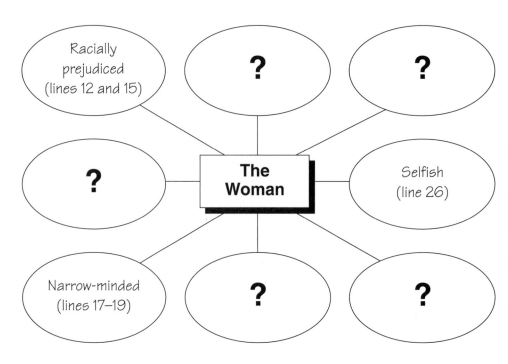

Try to include eight qualities of her character which come out in the poem. If you find more, add them.

For each quality you identify, put down a line number from the poem which gives evidence to back up your choice.

The poem   Read the poem below to yourself, twice.

It was written during the Second World War, when London was being bombed heavily. The woman speaking in the poem has gone into Westminster Abbey to pray for the nation's safety.

On your first reading, check the meaning of quite a number of words and references. These are given at the end of the poem. The second time through, try to hear inside your head the woman's accent and the tone of voice in which she is praying.

In Westminster Abbey

Let me take this other glove off
   As the *vox humana* swells,
And the beauteous **fields of Eden**
   Bask beneath the Abbey bells.
Here, **where England's statesmen lie**,   5
Listen to a lady's **cry**.

Gracious Lord, oh bomb the Germans.
   Spare their women for Thy Sake,
And if that is not too easy
   We will pardon Thy Mistake.   10
But, gracious Lord, **whate'er shall be**,
Don't let anyone bomb me.

Keep our Empire **undismembered**
   Guide our Forces by Thy Hand,
Gallant blacks from far **Jamaica**,   15
   Honduras and Togoland;
Protect them Lord in all their fights,
And, even more, protect the whites.

Think of what our Nation stands for,
   Books from Boots' and country lanes,   20
Free speech, free passes, class distinction,
   Democracy and proper drains.
Lord, put beneath Thy special care
One-eighty-nine Cadogan Square.

Although dear Lord I am a sinner,   25
   I have done no major crime;
Now I'll come to Evening Service
   Whensoever I have the time.
So, Lord, reserve for me a **crown**,
And do not let my shares go down.   30

I will labour for Thy Kingdom,
   Help our lads to win the war,
Send white feathers to the cowards,
   Join the Women's Army **Corps**,
Then wash the Steps around Thy Throne   35
In the Eternal Safety Zone.

Now I feel a little better,
   What a treat to hear Thy Word,
Where the bones of leading statesmen
   Have so often been **interr'd**.   40
And now, dear Lord, I cannot wait
Because I have a luncheon date.

JOHN BETJEMAN

vox humana: organ music
fields of Eden: to the woman, the fields of England are like Paradise
Bask: sleep peacefully
where England's statesmen lie: many famous English politicians are buried here
cry: prayer
whate'er shall be: whatever happens
undismembered: unharmed, united
Jamaica, Honduras and Togoland: these three countries were part of the British Empire
Books from Boots': Boots' the Chemist used to run a lending library
One-eighty-nine Cadogan Square: the woman's own address
crown: place in Heaven
Corps: pronounced 'core'
interr'd: buried, laid to rest

Post-reading activities on 'In Westminster Abbey'

ACTIVITY 3	*Character profile (2)*

With a partner, make a 'character gram' to describe the woman who is speaking in the poem. Follow exactly the same instructions as for Activity 2, working with the same partner.

Compare your character grams of the two women. In how many ways are they alike? Have you found any major differences between them?

Look through some glossy magazines and colour supplements. Find a picture which looks like your idea of the woman in 'When the Bomb Drops' and one which matches your image of the woman in 'In Westminster Abbey'.

Cut these out, stick them on to your character grams, and display them.

ACTIVITY 4	*Satire, juxtaposition and rhyme*

Form a small group. Both these poems are **satires** – that is, they make fun of (or ridicule) the two women. The poets do this with 'tongue-in-cheek', but their purpose is actually a serious one.

One way in which they satirise the women is by the use they make of **juxtaposition** and **rhyme**. Juxtaposition literally means 'putting next to'. For example, you might say: 'Great video – shame about the song' or 'He's a terrific goalkeeper. Is there no beginning to his talent?' In each case, you are being satirical by putting two phrases next to each other which don't 'fit' or match up, and which therefore make a serious joke.

Look together at these extracts from 'In Westminster Abbey':

✧ 'Gracious Lord, oh bomb the Germans' (line 7).

✧ 'Free speech, free passes, class distinction' (line 21).

✧ 'Now I feel a little better,
   What a treat to hear Thy Word' (lines 37–38).

Discuss how John Betjeman's use of juxtaposition in these quotations makes a serious joke at the woman's expense.

The use of juxtaposition for the purpose of ridicule is often made stronger by rhyme. Look together at these pairs of rhyming lines (called **couplets**):

✧ 'Protect them Lord in all their fights,
   And, even more, protect the whites' (lines 17–18).

63

❖ 'So, Lord, reserve for me a crown,
And do not let my shares go down' (lines 29–30)

❖ 'And now, dear Lord, I cannot wait
Because I have a luncheon date' (lines 41–42).

Discuss how the rhymes in these quotations serve to bring out even more the serious jokes Betjeman is making about the woman.

ACTIVITY 5   *Women in wartime: a man's view*

Read the poem below, written by a British soldier during the First World War. It is a fierce satire on women's attitudes to war, as the poet sees them.

Glory of Women

You love us when we're heroes, home on leave,
Or wounded in a mentionable place.
You worship **decorations**; you believe
That **chivalry redeems** the war's disgrace.
You make us shells. You listen with delight,   5
By tales of dirt and danger fondly thrilled.
You crown our **distant ardours** while we fight,
And mourn our **laurelled** memories when we're killed.
You can't believe that British troops 'retire'
When hell's last horror breaks them, and they run,   10
Trampling the terrible corpses – blind with blood.
   O German mother dreaming by the fire,
   While you are knitting socks to send your son
   His face is trodden deeper in the mud.

SIEGFRIED SASSOON

decorations: medals won for bravery in battle
chivalry: the concept of heroism
redeems: justifies
distant ardours: supreme efforts on foreign battlefields
laurelled: the Romans gave laurel-wreaths to their dead warriors
retire: retreat in the face of the enemy

Think through your own response to this poem by discussing, as a whole class, the questions which follow.

Understanding

According to Siegfried Sassoon:

✧ What do women 'love', 'worship' and take 'delight' in during wartime?

✧ What do women find it impossible to believe about war? Why?

✧ In what ways are women, including the 'German mother', both ignorant and misguided about the realities of war?

Response

✧ What is your understanding of the poem's title? In what respects is it a satirical one?

✧ How many times does Sassoon address women in general directly, as if speaking to them face-to-face, with the word 'you'? Is this form of direct address effective for the poem's purpose?

✧ Why do you think Sassoon introduces a German woman at the end of the poem? Do you find the contrast made in the last two lines an effective one?

✧ Where in the poem is Sassoon's tone most

    sarcastic   ironic   angry   sympathetic?

✧ How do the last six lines (beginning 'You can't believe…') contrast with the first eight? In your opinion, is this contrast successful?

Form a small group. You have been invited to take part in a 15-minute TV discussion programme, 'Fire Back'. In it you have the chance to support or criticise Sassoon's views about women in wartime.

Appoint a chairperson. Everyone else appears as themselves.

Before you start, you may find it helpful to consider whether:

✧ women contribute more in wartime than knitting socks.

✧ women only love heroes.

✧ women suffer during a war.

✧ women are as naïve about war as Sassoon claims.

✧ women think of war in terms of its supposed 'glory'.

Now hold your discussion. Since you are simulating a TV programme, it would be ideal if your discussion could be video-taped.

End-of-unit further writing suggestions

On your own:

a Look back to Activity 1. Put yourself in the place of three of the people you thought should be in the nuclear shelter. Write a 'Note to the World' from each of them explaining exactly why they deserve to survive.

b Imagine that the two women speakers in 'When the Bomb Drops' and 'In Westminster Abbey' live at the same time. They meet at a dinner-party.

Write the conversation they have with each other. Include their feelings about:

✧ their country.

✧ foreigners.

✧ religion.

✧ their friends and families.

✧ themselves and their way of life.

✧ anything else you think would be of mutual interest to them.

Take your cue for the way they speak from the poems in this unit.

c It is sometimes said that nowadays the threat of nuclear war is over, or, at least, that it is far less serious than it was when you were born. Do you agree?

Write your views on this issue in one of the following forms:

✧ a short pamphlet entitled 'The Nuclear Threat Today: Myth or Reality?'

✧ a script for your appearance on a 5-minute TV programme, 'Soapbox', to give a personal opinion about the matter.

✧ a letter to a newspaper the day after a front-page story has appeared with the headline 'The West Accelerates Nuclear Wind-Down'.

Write in a style suitable to whichever of these forms you choose.

The loss of love

Neutral Tones   THOMAS HARDY

Absence   ELIZABETH JENNINGS

The two poems in this unit are written by people who were deeply in love but whose relationships ended in break-up.

Thomas Hardy writes about the reasons why this happened to him and reflects on how he was affected by it. Elizabeth Jennings also looks back on her emotional loss but is more concerned with the extent to which she has recovered from it.

Each poem expresses strong feeling. As you work through this unit, you will see how personal emotions are often most effectively conveyed by writers who use poetic technique to order their feelings, and so make them comprehensible to us. In particular, you will become aware of the way Thomas Hardy and Elizabeth Jennings employ the device of **symbolism** to achieve this effect.

$\mathscr{P}$*re-reading activity on both poems*

Breaking up

Form a small group. The majority of popular songs are about people falling, or being, in love. Most of the rest are about people falling, or being, *out* of it. Do they tell the truth about life as it really is?

Below is a list of ten possible reasons why teenagers' relationships break up. They are in no particular order.

A One partner finds another who is more physically and/or emotionally attractive.

B There is a reluctance to become too involved with just one person, combined with a wish to 'play the field'.

C The disapproval or interference of parents puts an unbearable strain on the relationship.

D After getting to know the other partner better, s/he turns out to be far less attractive than s/he first seemed.

E One or both partners develop new or different outside interests which occupy a good deal of their time and start to push them apart.

F One partner becomes over-possessive of the other.

G The partners spend more and more time in petty bickering, leading to almost continual rows.

H Sheer boredom: the relationship fizzles out because it has grown too predictable and stale.

I The relationship is undermined by friends of one or both partners making fun, being jealous, spreading rumours, cutting the partner(s) out of their 'crowd', etc.

J One of the partners is discovered by the other to be 'two-timing'.

Drawing on your own direct or indirect experience, try to agree on an order of priority from this list to explain why relationships break up. If you think, for example, that **D** is the most common reason and that **H** is the least common, write on a sheet of paper **D** = 1, **H** = 10, and so on.

Join up with another group and compare opinions. If there are major differences, discuss why. Add other points you think ought to have been in the list and 'rank order' them with those that are.

The poem Read the poem below twice, once to yourself, using the glossary, then aloud with a partner. On the second reading, take it in turns to read alternate stanzas. It is a mournful, and in some ways bitter, poem: try to bring out this mood by the tone and speed with which you read it.

It was written in 1867, when its author was twenty-seven. He is looking back to the precise moment when he realised that a girl he loved passionately had lost her love for him.

Neutral Tones

We stood by a pond that winter day,
And the sun was white, as though **chidden of** God,
And a few leaves lay on the starving **sod**;
   – They had fallen from an ash, and were gray.

Your eyes on me were as eyes that rove   5
Over tedious riddles of years ago;
And some words played between us to and fro
    On which lost the more by our love.

The smile on your mouth was the deadest thing
Alive enough to have strength to die;   10
And a grin of bitterness swept **thereby**
    Like an ominous bird **a-wing**…

Since then, **keen** lessons that love deceives,
And **wrings** with wrong, have shaped to me
Your face, and the God-curst sun, and a tree,   15
    And a pond edged with grayish leaves.

THOMAS HARDY

chidden of: scolded or rebuked by ('chidden' is the past tense of the verb 'to chide')
sod: earth, ground
thereby: i.e. across the girl's mouth
a-wing: in flight
keen: sharp, bitter
wrings: painfully tortures

Post-reading activities on 'Neutral Tones'

ACTIVITY 2   *The reasons why*

Work with a partner. What does the poem tell us about *why* Hardy's relationship ended? You need to read stanzas 2 and 3 intensively to find the answer. This lies not only in the 'surface meaning' of the poem but also in the style in which Hardy has chosen to write it.

The questions below will help you to arrive at your own explanation. Make notes as you discuss and answer them:

✧ How does the girl look at Hardy, exactly? What is suggested about her feelings by the fact that her eyes seem to 'rove'?

✧ If the girl finds looking at Hardy like returning to 'tedious riddles of years ago', what are her present feelings likely to be? Do you think she has always felt like this?

✧ When the couple speak, 'some words played between us'. What is implied about their conversation by the fact that it is made up only of 'some words'? What does Hardy suggest about how they talk by saying that these words 'played' between them?

✧ The girl does not express anger or hatred: she *smiles* at Hardy. How does he know, however, that her smile is a false one and not an expression of genuine pleasure in his company? How can a smile be 'the deadest thing'?

✧ What impression do you think Hardy is trying to convey by the simile comparing the girl's smile which 'swept' across her face with an 'ominous bird' in flight?

ACTIVITY 3   *The symbolic setting (1)*

Work with the same partner as you had for Activity 2. Almost half of Hardy's poem is given over to a description of the place where he realised that his relationship with the girl was over.

The questions that follow ask you to connect the poet's description of place, or **setting**, with his feelings of loss. Hardy's purpose is to use a **pattern of symbols** to tell us more about these feelings (that is, to use the details of the scene to reflect his own emotional state).

As you talk together, keep careful notes of what you say.

In what ways is it symbolically appropriate that:

✧ the poem has a winter setting?

✧ the only colours in the poem are pale white and grey?

✧ the sun seems to be weak, lacking in either light or warmth?

✧ there are only a 'few leaves' on the ground?

✧ the leaves are grey and have 'fallen' from an ash tree?

✧ the earth is described as 'starving'?

✧ the title of the poem is 'Neutral Tones'?

The pattern of symbolism you have been tracing is carefully and deliberately created by Hardy. Show this to be true by explaining the final two lines of the poem.

ACTIVITY 4   *Other aspects of style*

With the same partner, look again at the last stanza. In its opening line, Hardy sums up in two words his disillusioned, bitter feelings – not only about this particular relationship but also about love in general: 'love deceives'.

The style of the last stanza is intended to underline this bleak conclusion. Discuss how it does so by answering the following questions.

✧ How does the **alliterative** sound of the phrase 'wrings with wrong' reinforce its meaning?

✧ How is the central symbol of Hardy's disillusionment, the girl's face, given emphasis by the **verse structure**?

✧ What is the difference between the phrase 'chidden of God' (stanza 1) and 'God-curst' (stanza 4) to describe the sun?

✧ Which of the following words accurately describe the rhythm of the last two lines, and which do not?

      lively   disjointed   smooth   brisk   halting

      lifeless   faltering   vigorous   slow-moving

Is the rhythm of the closing lines appropriate to what they describe?

The poem   Read the poem below to yourself, twice – once to form a general understanding of its theme and once to make a few initial comparisons with 'Neutral Tones'. Elizabeth Jennings is writing about 100 years after Hardy.

Absence

I visited the place where we last met.
Nothing was changed, the gardens were well-tended,
The fountains sprayed their usual steady jet;
There was no sign that anything had ended
And nothing to instruct me to forget.   5

The thoughtless birds that shook out of the trees,
Singing an ecstasy I could not share,
Played cunning in my thoughts. Surely in these
Pleasures there could not be a pain to bear
Or any discord shake the level breeze.   10

It was because the place was just the same
That made your absence seem a savage force,
For under all the gentleness there came
An earthquake tremor: fountain, birds and grass
Were shaken by my thinking of your name.   15

ELIZABETH JENNINGS

Post-reading activity on 'Absence'

_____
ACTIVITY 5   *Statementing the poem*

Form a small group. Unlike Hardy, Elizabeth Jennings does not describe how or why her relationship ended. Rather, she is concerned with the pain of remembering her love for someone who is now 'absent' from her life.

In order to clarify what we are being told in the poem, consider as a group the following statements about it. Say whether you think each statement is:

A Completely true.

B Completely untrue.

C Only partly true.

Before you commit yourselves, you will need to find convincing evidence from the poem to back up your opinion.

The statements are numbered. On a sheet of paper, show what you think by writing, for example: 1 = **B**, 2 = **A**, and so on.

1   Elizabeth Jennings forces herself to revisit 'the place where we last met' to try to come to terms with the break-up of her relationship.

2   She is reassured, and made to feel less upset, by the fact that 'the place' is unchanged.

3   As she becomes aware of the carefree birds singing in the trees, she starts to feel almost happy again.

4   She realises that, although the relationship is over, life must go on. There is no point in dwelling on the past.

5   If the place she revisits had been different from the last time she met there with her lover, she would have felt less distressed about the break-up.

6   She is surprised to find how much love she still feels for the person who is no longer part of her life.

7   The whole poem is a sentimental wallowing in her feelings of loss. Elizabeth Jennings is deliberately, and unnecessarily, putting herself through the pain of trying to re-live a relationship that is best forgotten.

8   The poem is entitled 'Absence' because love, rather than her lover, has gone. She has been 'in love with love' rather than with one particular person.

$\mathcal{P}$*ost-reading activities on both poems*

ACTIVITY 6   *The symbolic setting (2)*

Work with a partner. Both poems in this unit focus closely on particular places. Like Hardy, Elizabeth Jennings uses the setting of her poem to create a **pattern of symbols** which reflect her various feelings.

Discuss, and make notes about, the ways in which it is symbolically appropriate that:

✧ the gardens are neat, tidy and well kept.

✧ the fountains are playing 'their usual steady jet'.

- ✧ the birds are 'thoughtless' and 'singing an ecstasy' (that is, singing in a joyful way).

- ✧ the breeze is 'level' (that is, steady and calm, the opposite of a turbulent, gusty wind).

- ✧ at the end of the poem, the fountain, the birds and the neatly-cut lawns are all 'shaken' by 'an earthquake tremor'.

Now compare Elizabeth Jennings's use of symbolic setting with Hardy's. Which do you find the more successful, and why?

ACTIVITY 7   *Written assignment*

On your own, draw on the notes you have made throughout this unit to undertake the following task. As you comment on both poems, ensure that you use quotations from the text to illustrate the key points you make.

> Write a comparative analysis of 'Neutral Tones' and 'Absence', bringing out the two poets' feelings about 'the loss of love' and commenting on the style in which they express these feelings. Say, with reasons, which poem you feel is the more effective in achieving its author's intentions.

End-of-unit further writing suggestions

On your own:

a Write your own poem, or sequence of poems, on the theme of 'The Loss of Love' and/or 'The Learning of Love'.

b Draft a one-page description of an outdoor or indoor setting which you associate strongly with one of these emotions:

peacefulness	stress	triumph	anger
loneliness	danger	anxiety	grief

Then write a real-life or imagined story in which the setting you have described plays a central part. The events and characters in your story are up to you to decide.

As in 'Neutral Tones' and 'Absence', use your setting to reflect the dominant emotions in your writing.

c One of the poems in this unit is written from a man's point of view; the other from a woman's.

In your opinion, do the two sexes have fundamentally different attitudes towards their relationships with each other? It may be that your reading, as well as your own observation and experience, has helped you towards the conclusion you have reached.

Make clear your feelings on this question by writing a story, a playscript or a discussion essay, the precise content of which you are free to determine.

d Look back to the list of possible reasons why relationships break up, which you considered in Activity 1.

Select one statement from this list. Use it as the basis for a story, real or imagined, in which you concentrate on:

✧ bringing out clearly the characters of those involved and the way their feelings change.

✧ including dialogue (i.e. conversation) in your story that is typical of real life rather than of a 'soap opera'.

✧ choosing settings which reflect the feelings of your main characters.

✧ working towards an ending which makes clear not only how, but also why, the central relationship in your story reaches the point it does.

Before Agincourt   WILLIAM SHAKESPEARE

The Send-off   WILFRED OWEN

The subject of this unit is 'going to war'.

Two quite different viewpoints about the rights and wrongs of warfare are given. The first is taken from one of Shakespeare's most 'military' plays, *Henry V*. King Henry is about to lead his troops into battle. He speaks eloquently to them about the honour and glory to be gained from fighting.

Wilfred Owen's poem, 'The Send-off', is set 500 years later in the First World War. It challenges the idea that there is any honour at all in fighting for one's country.

Working through this unit will help you make up your own mind on the matter. You will also learn something about the way in which **language**, **verse form** and other aspects of **style** have the power to persuade you to accept – or at least to understand – a point of view which you may not share.

Pre-reading activity on both poems

ACTIVITY 1 *Answering the call*

Form a small group. If war were to be declared five years from now, would *you* be prepared to 'do your bit' for Queen and Country, in whatever capacity?

As a way of opening out your discussion on this subject, first read the poem below. It is actually a song urging young men to join up and fight at the Front Line just after the outbreak of the First World War in 1914. It was sung by groups of young women on the music hall stages of the time.

We Don't Want To Lose You...

We've watched you playing cricket
And every kind of game,
At football, golf and polo
You men have made your name;
But now your Country calls you
To play your part in War,
And no matter what befalls you,
We shall love you all the more.
So – come and join the forces,
As your fathers did before.

Oh, we don't want to lose you,
But we think you ought to go,
For your King and your Country
Both need you so.
We shall want you, and miss you,
But with all our might and mane
We shall cheer you – thank you – kiss you
When you come home again.

In a five-minute discussion, brainstorm all the ways in which this song – which was immensely effective in persuading civilians to enlist – uses techniques of persuasion to make young men feel that they 'ought to go' to war. Try to identify at least five points.

Whatever your personal feelings on the matter, imagine that you are a totally committed pacifist. You would refuse to fight, or to help with the war effort, under *any* circumstances. What might your reasons be? In discussion, try to come up with at least five strong arguments against participating in war.

Join up with another group and conduct a fifteen-minute debate on this question. Group **A** is in favour of fighting for Queen and Country, Group **B** is against. Appoint someone to take the minutes of your discussion.

The poem   Read the extract below to yourself. It is taken from Shakespeare's *Henry V*. Keep
referring to the glossary at the end of the extract.

Context

*It is 1415. At the head of the English army fighting against France, King
Henry V, having captured a number of French towns and cities, now faces
serious problems. His army has been decimated by illness, a shortage of
food, and some desertion. The soldiers are battle-weary. It is vital that
the English take the town of Agincourt to press home their advantage,
but the French forces greatly outnumber the English and are
strategically much better placed.*

*Henry's generals, the Earl of Westmoreland in particular, can see that
they are facing near-certain defeat. At the start of this extract, he
voices the wish that they had reinforcements from England to boost
their numbers. Henry's task is to motivate his exhausted and depleted
army to fight for their country against overwhelming odds – and to win.*

Before Agincourt

Westmoreland. O! that we now had here
    But one ten thousand of those men in England
    That do no work to-day.

King Henry.   What's he that wishes so?
    My cousin Westmoreland? No, my fair cousin: 5
    If we are **mark'd** to die, **we are enow**
    To do our country loss; and, if to live,
    The fewer men, the greater share of honour.
    God's will! I pray thee, wish not one man more.
    By Jove, I am not **covetous for gold**,   10
    Nor care I who doth **feed upon my cost**;
    It yearns me not if men my garment wear;
    Such outward things dwell not in my desires:
    But if it be a sin to **covet** honour,
    I am the most **offending** soul alive.   15
    No, faith, my coz, wish not a man from England:
    God's peace! I would not lose so great an honour
    As one man more, methinks, would share from me,
    For the best hope I have. O! do not wish one more:
    Rather proclaim it, Westmoreland, through **my host**,   20
    That he which hath no stomach to this fight,
    Let him depart; **his passport shall be made**,
    And **crowns** for convoy put into his purse:

We would not die in that man's company
That fears his fellowship to die with us.   25
This day is call'd the feast of **Crispian**:
He that outlives this day, and comes safe home,
Will stand a tip-toe when this day is nam'd,
And **rouse him** at the name of Crispian.
He that shall live this day, and see old age,   30
Will yearly on the **vigil** feast his neighbours,
And say, 'To-morrow is Saint Crispian:'
Then will he strip his sleeve and show his scars,
And say, 'These wounds I had on Crispian's day.'
Old men forget: yet all shall be forgot,   35
But he'll remember **with advantages**
What **feats** he did that day. Then shall our names,
Familiar in his mouth as household words,
Harry the king, Bedford and Exeter,
Warwick and Talbot, Salisbury and **Gloucester**,   40
Be in their flowing cups freshly remember'd.
This story shall the good man teach his son;
And Crispin Crispian shall **ne'er go by**,
From this day to the ending of the world,
But we in it shall be remembered;   45
We few, we happy few, we band of brothers;
For he to-day that sheds his blood with me
Shall be my brother; be he **ne'er so vile**
This day shall gentle his condition:
And gentlemen in England, now a-bed,   50
Shall think themselves accurs'd they were not here,
And **hold their manhoods cheap** whiles any speaks
That fought with us upon Saint Crispin's day.

WILLIAM SHAKESPEARE

mark'd: intended by God
we are enow: we are men enough/there are enough of us
covetous for gold: greedy for wealth
feed upon my cost: gain financially by capturing me in battle and receiving a
    ransom for my release
covet: crave, wish for
offending: sinful
my host: the soldiers in my army
his passport shall be made: he will be allowed safe passage to leave the
    battlefield and return to England
crowns: golden coins
Crispian: a Saint's Day – Saint Crispian (or Crispin) was a Roman martyr
rouse him: swell with pride

vigil: the evening before
with advantages: with praise from those who hear his story
feats: brave deeds
…*Gloucester*: a list of Henry's generals, all Lords and Earls
ne'er go by: never be allowed to pass
ne'er so vile: however lowly in status he is
hold their manhoods cheap: think of themselves as lacking in manliness

Post-reading activities on 'Before Agincourt'

ACTIVITY 2   *Persuasions*

Form a small group. Before beginning this activity, it would be a great help if you could see on video the extract you have just read. There are two film versions of *Henry V*, one starring Laurence Olivier, and a more recent one starring Kenneth Branagh.

Re-read King Henry's speech from line 26 ('This day is call'd the feast of Crispian') to the end. Each of you should make a 'note chart' listing all the things Henry says to persuade his soldiers to fight and to fill them with confidence. It is important that you use your own words.

Do it like this:

Line	Reasons for fighting
27–28	All those who survive and return to England will feel immense pride whenever the anniversary of the battle comes round

| 50–53 | In the future, men who did **not** fight at Agincourt will envy those who did, and think themselves inferior in manliness |

Look for about eight separate points to enter on your charts.

ACTIVITY 3   *Doubts and reservations*

With a partner, imagine you are two soldiers in Henry's army who are not convinced by his rousing speech. Plan in note form a speech in reply to his, answering his 'persuasions' one by one and giving an alternative point of view. You might mention to Henry what he omitted to say.

Join up with another pair and compare notes. The purpose of this activity is not to actually *write* the soldiers' speech!

ACTIVITY 4   *The way that he says it*

Work with a partner.

Clearly, it is not only *what* King Henry says that sounds very persuasive. It is also the *style* in which he speaks. The purpose of this activity is to explore his speech style in greater detail.

You need to remind yourselves that Shakespeare normally wrote in blank verse (i.e. poetry that does not rhyme but which has five strong 'beats' to every line). For example:

> That fought with us upon Saint Crispin's day.
> v———// v—// v—// v———// v—//

To gain the effects that he wants, Shakespeare's use of the placing of words for emphasis in a blank verse line, of certain kinds of rhythm and of repetition, are all-important. Examine these in turn:

The placing of words

Look again at lines 27–34 (ending '…Crispian's day') and at lines 43 to the end of the whole speech.

Take it in turns to read these passages aloud. Then imagine you are directing an actor to speak them as dramatically as possible. Working line by line, list on a sheet of paper all the words you would want him to give special emphasis to, so that Henry's persuasive tactics come over really strongly.

Rhythm

Look again at lines 15–26 and lines 32–42.

Take it in turns to read the passages aloud. Which of these words are suitable to describe the rhythm of the lines, and which are not?

   hesitant   fast-paced   confident   fragmented   flowing

   bold   downbeat   swelling   subdued   forceful

Discuss why the rhythm you have now identified is appropriate to what Henry is saying.

Repetition

Throughout Henry's speech, he repeats certain words and phrases quite frequently. Look carefully for them. For what reasons do you think Henry chooses to highlight them by repetition?

The poem
Read the poem below once to yourself, then once aloud with a partner. The second time through, read alternate stanzas, using a suitable tone of voice.

The poem is, like the extract from *Henry V*, about a group of soldiers who are being 'called to arms'. However, the circumstances they find themselves in are very different. The poem is set during the First World War. The scene is somewhere in England. A platoon of new recruits, recently trained for combat at a remote army camp in the countryside, is being boarded onto a military train. They will be transported to the south coast, shipped across the Channel, and then sent to fight at the front line in France. They have no idea exactly where they are going, nor of what awaits them in the trenches.

The Send-off

Down the close darkening lanes they sang their way
To the **siding-shed**,
And lined the train with faces grimly gay.

Their breasts were stuck all white with **wreath and spray**
As men's are, dead.   5

Dull porters watched them, and a casual tramp
Stood staring hard,
Sorry to miss them from the **upland camp**.

Then, unmoved, signals nodded, and a lamp
Winked to the guard.   10

So secretly, like wrongs hushed-up, they went.
They were not ours:
We never heard to which front these were sent;

Nor there if they yet mock what women meant
Who gave them flowers.   15

Shall they return to beatings of great bells
In wild train-loads?
A few, a few, too few for drums and yells,
May creep back, silent, to village wells,
Up half-known roads.   20

WILFRED OWEN

From *The Poems of Wilfred Owen*, ed. J. Stallworthy, Chatto & Windus, 1985.

siding-shed: the part of the railway station where the soldiers will board the
   train
wreath and spray: flowers given to the soldiers to celebrate their send-off –
   they have stuck them in their tunics
upland camp: the army training camp where the recruits have been stationed
They were not ours: they did not belong to the same regiment as Wilfred Owen.
   (Owen was himself an officer during the war. He was killed in action in
   1918, aged 25.)

Post-reading activities on 'The Send-off'

| ACTIVITY 5 | *Text search* |

Work with a partner. 'The Send-off' is perhaps the most 'compressed' poem in
this volume. It could be said to tell the story of the First World War, or at least
one version of it, in twenty lines of verse. This being so, it is necessary to search
the text in some detail before the poem gives up its full meaning.

Use the following questions to help you understand the text, each making notes
as you decide on your answers.

✧ What mood do you think the soldiers are in as they march to the station, and
   afterwards as they line the train (stanza 1)?

✧ What point is Owen making about the flowers which decorate the soldiers'
   tunics by his use of the simile in line 5?

✧ Who will miss the soldiers when they have been sent off to the war (stanza 3)?
   What do you think Owen's purpose is in making a point of telling us this?

✧ What do you think Owen is implying about the way the soldiers are sent to
   fight by his simile in line 11?

✧ What sense do you make of the sixth stanza? Think particularly about the
   word 'mock'.

✧ In the last stanza, Owen asks if the soldiers will return from the war to a
   heroes' welcome in 'wild train-loads'. What answer does he give to his own
   question?

When you have finished, join up with another pair and compare your responses.

<u>ACTIVITY 6</u>   *Shades of meaning*

Work with the same partner as you had for Activity 5. Poets often choose words for their depth of meaning. This is not to say that they use 'hidden' meanings which need to be cracked like some impenetrable code. Rather, it is in the nature of language sometimes to suggest several shades of meaning at the same time.

With this in mind, discuss and make notes on Owen's use of the words to which the following questions draw your attention.

◇ What is implied about the soldiers' eventual destination by the fact that the lanes down which they march are 'close' and 'darkening' (line 1)?

◇ The soldiers depart from a 'siding-shed'. What does this suggest about the attitude of the military authorities towards the young recruits they send off to war?

◇ Why do you think Owen draws our attention to the fact that the flowers in the soldiers' tunics are 'wreath and spray'?

◇ The old-style wooden signals which are raised to give an all-clear to the train are 'unmoved' (line 9). What may Owen be telling us here?

◇ In the next line, the signal lamp 'winked' at the guard. Is there another shade of meaning here to add to 'flickered'?

◇ Why are the soldiers compared with 'wrongs' (line 11)?

◇ Imagining the soldiers returning home, Owen writes 'A few …may creep back' (lines 18–19). What does this suggest about the mental, as well as the physical, state they will be in if and when they *do* survive the war?

Post-reading activities on both poems

<u>ACTIVITY 7</u>   *Other aspects of style*

With the same partner, refer back to Activity 4 in this unit.

What examples can you find in 'The Send-off' of Owen using word-placement, rhythm and repetition to achieve his effects? Are they the same effects as those you identified in the speech by Henry V?

ACTIVITY 8   *Written commentary*

On your own, draw on the work you have done in the course of this unit to write a commentary with the following title:

> Contrast the attitudes towards fighting in war expressed by Shakespeare's *Henry V* and Wilfred Owen. Show how the way in which each poem is written serves to bring out these attitudes very clearly.

It is vital that you use frequent quotation to support the points you make in your commentary.

End-of-unit further writing suggestions

On your own:

a Imagine that this country has become drawn into another war similar to that in the Falkland Islands or the Gulf.

Produce a pamphlet which *either* encourages people to support the war effort *or* urges them to oppose it. Use whatever written and graphical techniques of persuasion you feel are most effective to your purpose.

b Write a review of any book, film or TV programme you have read or seen which has strongly influenced your own feelings about war.

The review should explain why and in what ways it made an impact on you: do not be content only to describe the 'plot'.

Why would you recommend other people to read or see it?

c Conduct a number of interviews with people who have experienced war personally, either as participants or as civilians.

What were their experiences? What are their views, and how do these compare with your own? Tape record, or make notes about, the interviews.

Present your research in written form under the title 'At First Hand'. Your aims are:

✧ to reflect accurately the experiences recounted to you, making a selection which avoids repetition.

✧ to represent fairly the views about war you have heard, ensuring that you do not include only those which match your own.

✧ to write in a style suitable for an intelligent adult reader.

10 *Natural or unnatural endings?*

The Need of Being Versed in Country Things
ROBERT FROST

Depopulation of the Hills
R. S. THOMAS

Both poems in this unit concern the relationship between man and nature. This has been a favourite subject for poets since at least the early 1800s. However, Robert Frost, who was a farmer in America, and R. S. Thomas, a parson in a rural area of mid-Wales, approach the subject differently from traditional English 'nature poets' such as Wordsworth.

In these poems, nature causes destruction. As you work through the unit, you will be looking closely at how the poets' **style** helps to convey their views about man in the context of nature's world – a world which can be both hospitable and hostile to human beings.

The poem Read the poem on this page twice, once to yourself, then once aloud with a partner. The second time through, take it in turns to read alternate stanzas, adopting a suitable pace, rhythm and tone of voice.

The Need of Being Versed in Country Things

The house had gone to bring again
To the midnight sky a sunset glow.
Now the chimney was all of the house that stood,
Like a pistil after the petals go.

The barn opposed across the way,   5
That would have joined the house in flame
Had it been the will of the wind, was left
To bear forsaken the place's name.

No more it opened with all one end
For teams that came by the stony road   10
To drum on the floor with scurrying hoofs
And brush the **mow** with the summer load.

The birds that came to it through the air
At broken windows flew out and in,
Their murmur more like the sigh we sigh   15
From too much dwelling on what has been.

Yet for them the lilac renewed its leaf,
And the aged elm, though touched with fire;
And the dry pump flung up an awkward arm;
And the fence post carried a strand of wire.   20

For them there was nothing really sad.
But though they rejoiced in the nest they kept,
One had **to be versed in country things**
Not to believe the **phoebes** wept.

ROBERT FROST

mow: the hay already stored in the barn at harvest time
to be versed in country things: to understand the ways of nature
phoebes: small birds, native to North America

Post-reading activities on 'The Need of Being Versed in Country Things'

ACTIVITY 1   *'The house had gone...'*

With a partner, discuss the questions below. As you talk, you should each make careful notes about what you say. Use line numbers to illustrate the points you make.

What evidence is there in the poem to indicate:

✧ a farmhouse has burned down?

✧ the extent of the damage caused?

✧ what the farm was like in its heyday, before the fire?

✧ the reaction of the birds to the ruin of the farm?

ACTIVITY 2   *Aspects of style (1)*

With the same partner as you had for Activity 1, relate the poem's style to your understanding of its meaning as you discuss, and make notes about, the following:

✧ How does the opening half-line of the poem suggest that the fire destroyed the farmhouse very rapidly?

✧ Explain fully the simile in lines 3 and 4. What is being compared with what? In how many ways do you find this an appropriate simile to describe what has taken place?

✧ Look carefully again at stanza 3. What do you notice about the punctuation in this stanza? How does Frost's use of rhythm and the sound of words reinforce the impression of life on the farm as it was before the fire?

✧ Comment on the choice of the word 'murmur' to describe the birds' first reaction to the destruction of the farm. How does the simile in lines 15 and 16 connect the feelings of nature with the feelings of human beings?

✧ 'For them there was nothing really sad' (line 21). Look carefully again at stanza 5 to explain *why* this is the case for the birds. Note and comment on Frost's technique of listing in this stanza to convey his point.

✧ Consider the last stanza. What conclusion about the destruction of the farm does Frost come to, and how does this reflect his carefully chosen title for the poem?

The poem   Read the poem once to yourself, using the glossary, then once aloud with a partner. The second time through, take it in turns to read alternate stanzas. Adopt a suitable tone of voice to bring out Thomas's anger towards the elements and his sympathy for the people who have suffered such hardship under nature's assault upon them.

Before looking at the poem on this page, you need to know that R. S. Thomas lives among the sparse population of hill farmers in central Wales. When this poem was written, the extremely severe weather conditions were driving more and more farmers off the land. Thomas was concerned that, as a result, the entire community was in danger of being destroyed.

Depopulation of the Hills

Leave it, leave it – the hole under the door
Was a mouth through which the rough wind spoke
Ever more sharply; the dank hand
Of age was busy on the walls
Scrawling in blurred **characters**   5
Messages of hate and fear.

Leave it, leave it – the cold rain began
At summer end – there is no road
Over the bog, and winter comes
With mud above the **axletree**.   10

Leave it, leave it – the rain dripped
Day and night from the patched roof
Sagging beneath its load of sky.

Did the earth help them, time befriend
These last survivors? Did the spring grass   15
Heal winter's ravages? The grass
Wrecked them in its draughty tides,
Grew from the chimney-stack like smoke,
Burned its way through the weak timbers.
That was nature's jest, the sides   20
Of the **old hulk** cracked, but not with mirth.

R. S. Thomas

characters: written symbols, like hieroglyphs
axletree: rod connecting the wheels of a cart or other vehicle
old hulk: literally, a shipwreck; ramshackle farmhouse

Post-reading activities on 'Depopulation of the Hills'

ACTIVITY 3   *'Nature's jest…'*

With a partner, discuss, and make notes in answer to, the questions below about the fate of the Welsh hill farmers.

What evidence is there in the poem that:

✦ nature's elements are conducting a brutal campaign to drive the farmers out of their homes?

✦ the wind and rain, in particular, combine forces to terrorise the farmers and destroy their livelihood?

✦ the process of destruction is gradual but relentless?

✦ Thomas sees nature as a cruel tyrant, bent on spreading ruin rather than on preserving and renewing life?

ACTIVITY 4   *Aspects of style (2)*

With the same partner as you had for Activity 3, relate the poem's style to your understanding of its meaning as you discuss, and make notes about, the following:

✦ The first three stanzas begin in the same way: 'Leave it, leave it'. Who, or what, is speaking? Could 'leave it' have more than a single meaning?

✦ What might be a reason for the decreasing length of the first three stanzas?

✦ Look closely at the personifications in stanza 1. Explain how Thomas personifies the wind and time, suggesting reasons why he does so.

✦ What impressions are conveyed by 'the patched roof/Sagging beneath its load of sky' (lines 12–13)?

✦ Thomas begins the final stanza with two rhetorical questions (that is, questions which need no 'answer' because they answer themselves). What *is* the answer? How do you know?

✦ For what reasons is the grass compared, through Thomas's use of simile and metaphor, with the sea, smoke and fire (lines 17–19)? Why is this an unusual way for a 'nature poet' to describe grass?

✦ If it is 'nature's jest' to crack 'the sides of the old hulk' (lines 20–21), what view of nature does Thomas appear to be putting forward?

Post-reading activities on both poems

ACTIVITY 5   *In comparison*

Form a small group. These poems are similar in some ways and different in others. You should each make two 'note charts' to identify these similarities and differences. Include not only what happens in each poem but also the poets' attitudes to what they describe.

Try to put at least five points on each chart. Do it like this:

Similarities	
Robert Frost	**R. S. Thomas**
Farm destroyed by the elements of fire and wind	Farms destroyed by the elements of wind and rain
Human beings forced to leave – farm is reclaimed by nature	Human beings driven out by the elements – nature repossesses the land

Differences	
Contrasts life on the farm in the past with the desolation in the present	Only describes the process of ruin and decay taking place now – no other perspective
Takes a philosophical view of the changes nature brings about – saddened, but can understand it's part of the natural cycle of things	Very bitter about the changes nature brings about – angered, and cannot see any creative purpose in the natural cycle

ACTIVITY 6   *Written commentary*

On your own, use the notes you have made while working through this unit to write a commentary on both poems together, using the following title:

> Compare the way in which Frost and Thomas view nature and the effect it has on human life. Comment in detail on the style in which the poems are written, making clear how each poet's choice of language, use of simile and metaphor, verse structure, etc. helps to bring out his theme.

Upon Westminster Bridge WILLIAM WORDSWORTH

In a London Drawing-room MARY ANN EVANS

The two nineteenth-century poems in this unit present contrasting views of London. Wordsworth, writing in 1802, is struck by the beauty and grandeur of the city as dawn rises over it. Mary Ann Evans (better known for the novels she wrote under her pen-name 'George Eliot') portrays the capital fifty years later as a crowded, polluted place, the ugliness of which deadens the spirit of its inhabitants.

The contrast between the poems is underlined by the different forms in which they are written. 'Upon Westminster Bridge' is a **sonnet**, 'In a London Drawing-room' is written in **blank verse**. You will learn more about these forms and styles as you work through the unit.

Pre-reading activity on both poems

ACTIVITY 1   *Selling London*

As a class, look at the two pages printed below. They come from a 1996 tourist leaflet advertising the London Planetarium.

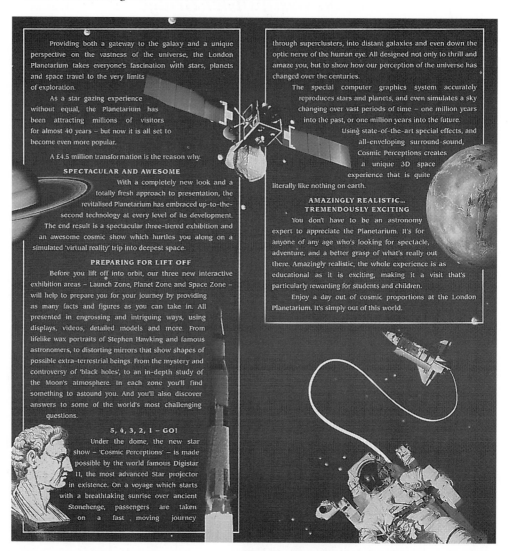

Providing both a gateway to the galaxy and a unique perspective on the vastness of the universe, the London Planetarium takes everyone's fascination with stars, planets and space travel to the very limits of exploration.

As a star gazing experience without equal, the Planetarium has been attracting millions of visitors for almost 40 years – but now it is all set to become even more popular.

A £4.5 million transformation is the reason why.

SPECTACULAR AND AWESOME

With a completely new look and a totally fresh approach to presentation, the revitalised Planetarium has embraced up-to-the-second technology at every level of its development. The end result is a spectacular three-tiered exhibition and an awesome cosmic show which hurtles you along on a simulated 'virtual reality' trip into deepest space.

PREPARING FOR LIFT OFF

Before you lift off into orbit, our three new interactive exhibition areas – Launch Zone, Planet Zone and Space Zone – will help to prepare you for your journey by providing as many facts and figures as you can take in. All presented in engrossing and intriguing ways, using displays, videos, detailed models and more. From lifelike wax portraits of Stephen Hawking and famous astronomers, to distorting mirrors that show shapes of possible extra-terrestrial beings. From the mystery and controversy of 'black holes', to an in-depth study of the Moon's atmosphere. In each zone you'll find something to astound you. And you'll also discover answers to some of the world's most challenging questions.

5, 4, 3, 2, 1 – GO!

Under the dome, the new star show – 'Cosmic Perceptions' – is made possible by the world famous Digistar II, the most advanced Star projector in existence. On a voyage which starts with a breathtaking sunrise over ancient Stonehenge, passengers are taken on a fast moving journey through superclusters, into distant galaxies and even down the optic nerve of the human eye. All designed not only to thrill and amaze you, but to show how our perception of the universe has changed over the centuries.

The special computer graphics system accurately reproduces stars and planets, and even simulates a sky changing over vast periods of time – one million years into the past, or one million years into the future. Using state-of-the-art special effects, and all-enveloping surround-sound, Cosmic Perceptions creates a unique 3D space experience that is quite literally like nothing on earth.

**AMAZINGLY REALISTIC...
TREMENDOUSLY EXCITING**

You don't have to be an astronomy expert to appreciate the Planetarium. It's for anyone of any age who's looking for spectacle, adventure, and a better grasp of what's really out there. Amazingly realistic, the whole experience is as educational as it is exciting, making it a visit that's particularly rewarding for students and children.

Enjoy a day out of cosmic proportions at the London Planetarium. It's simply out of this world.

Talk about the ways in which the leaflet tries to persuade people to visit the Planetarium. Include in your discussion the page layout, the use of illustrations, headings, variations in typeface and print size, and, in particular, the choice of language.

How effective do you judge this leaflet to be as a piece of advertising? Give specific reasons to support your opinion.

The poem Read the poem below to yourself, twice. On the first reading, picture as many details as possible of the scene Wordsworth is describing. The second time through, concentrate on Wordsworth's feelings as he looks across London in the early morning.

Upon Westminster Bridge

Earth has not anything to show more fair:
Dull would he be of soul who could pass by
A sight so touching in its majesty:
This City now doth, like a garment, wear   4
The beauty of the morning; silent, bare,
Ships, towers, domes, theatres, and temples lie
Open unto the fields, and to the sky;
All bright and glittering in the smokeless air.   8
Never did sun more beautifully **steep**
In his first splendour, valley, rock, or hill;
Ne'er saw I, never felt, a calm so deep!
The river glideth at his own sweet will:
Dear God! the very houses seem asleep;
And all that mighty heart is lying still!   14

WILLIAM WORDSWORTH

Earth has . . . more fair: there is no sight on earth more beautiful than this
steep: soak, or saturate, in sunlight

Post-reading activities on 'Upon Westminster Bridge'

ACTIVITY 2   *'This City now...'*

With a partner, make a quick but complete list of all the words and phrases in the poem which show that Wordsworth is describing London in the very early morning.

'Upon Westminster Bridge' was written about 200 years ago. Imagine you work for the Living History Museum Company which has re-created an experience of London as Wordsworth describes it. You offer trips back in time through your museum with sound effects and a commentary, as well as scaled-up models and 3D film sequences based on the details in the poem.

Use both your understanding of 'Upon Westminster Bridge' and your knowledge of London as it is today to draft an advertising leaflet for 'The 1802 London Time Travel Trip – buy your ticket now. Only £2.50 – it's well Wordsworth it!'

ACTIVITY 3   *City and country*

Wordsworth's best-known poems, which are set in the Lake District, usually describe the countryside rather than towns or cities.

In a small group, draw two columns, one headed 'Rural', the other headed 'Urban'. Then look again at the poem. Write in the appropriate column all the single words used by Wordsworth which you associate naturally with the countryside (rural), and with a city (urban).

What do you conclude from this activity about why Wordsworth finds such beauty in the London landscape he is describing?

The poem   Read the poem below, twice. First read it slowly to yourself. Then join up with a partner and read aloud its seven sentences turn by turn. Note that some sentences end in the middle of a line.

In a London Drawing-room

The sky is cloudy, yellowed by the smoke.
For view there are the houses opposite
Cutting the sky with one long line of wall
Like solid fog: far as the eye can stretch
Monotony of surface and of form   5
Without a break to hang a guess upon.
No bird can make a shadow as it flies,
For all its shadow, as in **ways** o'erhung
By thickest canvas, where the golden rays
Are clothed in **hemp**. No figure lingering   10
Pauses to feed the hunger of the eye
Or rest a little on the lap of life.
All hurry on and look upon the ground,
Or glance **unmarking** at the passers by.
The wheels are hurrying too, cabs, carriages   15
All closed, in multiplied identity.
The world seems one huge prison-house and **court**
Where men are punished at the slightest cost,
With lowest rate of colour, warmth and joy.

MARY ANN EVANS

ways: streets
hemp: thick fabric
unmarking: without seeing
court: i.e. a court of law

Post-reading activities on 'In a London Drawing-room'

ACTIVITY 4   *Particular meanings in context*

As a class, work towards a shared understanding of what Mary Ann Evans has in mind when she writes the following:

✧ 'Monotony of surface and of form
  Without a break to hang a guess upon' (lines 5–6).

✧ ' . . . the hunger of the eye' (line 11).

✧ 'Or rest a little on the lap of life' (line 12).

✧ 'All closed, in multiplied identity' (line 16).

✧ 'Where men are punished at the slightest cost' (line 18).

Why do you think:

✧ 'No bird can make a shadow . . . ' (line 7)?

✧ 'The world seems one huge prison-house . . . ' (line 17)?

ACTIVITY 5   *Overall impressions*

With a partner, draw four columns. Head three of them 'Colour', 'Sameness' and 'Speed of life'. Then look again at the poem. Write in the appropriate column all the words and phrases used by Mary Ann Evans which create the impressions that these headings describe.

What do you conclude from this activity about why Mary Ann Evans finds the London landscape she is describing so unpleasant?

Give the fourth column a heading of your own which denotes a further impression of London to be found in this poem. Enter any relevant quotations in this column.

Post-reading activities on both poems

Contrasting views

On your own, use the notes you have made on each poem to write a detailed account of the differences between the two poets' views of London.

Your account should cover both the details of the scenes the poets describe and their personal feelings about the city. Use quotations to illustrate every major point you make.

ACTIVITY 7 ## Forms of meaning

These two poems differ in their **form** as well as in the way they treat a common topic, London. The form of a poem is an essential part of its meaning; it is not just a 'garment' into which the poet chooses, at random, to fit his or her subject-matter.

The sonnet form

'Upon Westminster Bridge' is a sonnet: that is, it is fourteen lines long, has ten syllables to each line, and has a distinctive rhyming pattern (or rhyme scheme).

By yourself, look back at the poem and work out why the rhyme scheme can be summarised like this:

ABBA / ABBA / / CDCDCD

With a partner, read 'Upon Westminster Bridge' aloud, one person reading the first eight lines (or *octet*), the other person reading the last six lines (or *sestet*). Then draw two columns headed 'Octet: main impressions and key words' and 'Sestet: main impressions and key words'. Make notes in each column, working in as much detail as possible.

Use the notes you have made to discuss as a class how the things Wordsworth chooses to highlight in the octet differ from those he highlights in the sestet.

Consider how far there is a *contrast* and a *development* between the two parts of the sonnet. You should look not only at what Wordsworth describes but also at his choice of language, his tone, and the rhythm of the lines.

Blank verse

'In a London Drawing-room' is written in blank verse: that is, it has ten syllables to each line and is without a rhyme scheme of any kind. Shakespeare's plays are also written mainly in blank verse.

As a class, remind yourselves of Mary Ann Evans' main impressions of London in this poem. Then talk about why she may have chosen the blank verse form to convey these impressions by considering the questions below.

✧ Lines 2 to 5 are made up of a single sentence. There are no punctuation marks (and therefore no breaks) at the end of any of the lines. What effect does this have on the rhythm as you read? Is the rhythm appropriate to what is being described?

✧ In line 3, how does the sound of the phrase ' . . . with one long line of wall' echo its meaning? Ask the same question about the phrase ' . . . far as the eye can stretch' (line 4). In what respects do these two phrases sum up the poet's overall view of London?

✧ The third and fourth sentences of the poem begin in an identical way. What reasons can you suggest for this? How important is the word 'no' to the poem as a whole?

✧ Each of the lines has a total of ten syllables, but the length of the words within them varies a good deal. Pick out all the words which have three or four syllables and write them down. Taken together, how well do they characterise the mood or feeling of the whole poem?

✧ Mary Ann Evans uses a metaphor to round off her poem (see lines 17–19). Explain it in your own words. How fully would you say it represents the main themes of 'In a London Drawing-room'? Why do you think the last four words of the poem are 'colour, warmth and joy'?

ACTIVITY 8   *Form and style*

Write your own explanation of why Wordsworth chooses the sonnet form, whereas Mary Ann Evans chooses blank verse, to express their feelings about London. Draw fully on the work you have done in Activity 7 to help you decide what to write.

For further comparison

Below are two more pre-twentieth-century poems about London. They are suitable for comparing with the poems in this unit or with each other.

London

See what a mass of gems the city wears
Upon her broad live bosom! row on row
Rubies and emeralds and amethysts glow.
See! that huge circle, like a necklace, stares
With thousands of bold eyes to heaven, and dares
The golden stars to dim the lamps below
And in the mirror of the mire I know
The moon has left her image unawares.
That's the great town at night: I see her breasts,
Prick'd out with lamps they stand like huge black towers,
I think they move! I hear her panting breath.
And that's her head where the tiara rests.
And in her brain, through lanes as dark as death,
Men creep like thoughts . . . The lamps are like pale flowers.

LORD ALFRED DOUGLAS

London

I wander through each chartered street,
Near where the chartered Thames does flow.
And mark in every face I meet
Marks of weakness, marks of woe.

In every cry of every Man,
In every Infant's cry of fear,
In every voice, in every ban,
The mind-forged manacles I hear.

How the Chimney-sweeper's cry
Every blackening Church appalls;
And the hapless Soldier's sigh
Runs in blood down Palace walls.

But most through midnight streets I hear
How the youthful Harlot's curse
Blasts the new born Infant's tear,
And blights with plagues the Marriage hearse.

WILLIAM BLAKE

Heart of the matter

A Birthday CHRISTINA ROSSETTI

My Heart is Like a Withered Nut CAROLINE NORTON

In this unit, two female Victorian poets write about contrasting aspects of love: fulfilment and betrayal.

Christina Rossetti's poem celebrates both her own twenty-seventh birthday and 'the birthday of my life', since being in love for the first time makes her feel as though her real life is just beginning. By contrast, Caroline Norton, married for just five years, describes the anguish of being deserted by a husband she loved but who physically abused her and, after separating, refused to allow her any contact with their children.

Throughout this unit, you will be asked to make your own judgements about the poets' feelings and the way in which they express them.

Pre-reading activity on both poems

<u>ACTIVITY 1</u>   *One love: two versions*

With a partner, consider the way in which the following modern poem deals with the theme of love. Read the poem aloud, with one person reading the 'She' section and the other person reading the 'He' section. Then give your personal responses to the points on page 103, either as a pair or by contributing to a class discussion.

First Love

She:
I don't know why, but something's going wrong –
I felt the point of no return slip by.
Though we're still happy, we still get along

my heart beats like a toneless leaden gong
where once it leapt and raced as if to fly.
I don't know why. But something's going wrong

in me: the spark, the naturalness, has gone –
each day it's getting harder to deny;
though we're still happy, we still get along

I'm out of step. He hasn't changed. How long
each kiss feels with deceit; each touch a lie.
I don't know why, but something's going wrong.

I'd never felt such love – so fierce and strong:
each sight of him, each parting made me cry.
Though we're still happy, we still get along

the love that was to last a whole life long
is coming to an end. No second try,
though we're still happy, we still get along.
I don't know why, but something's going wrong.

He:
I knew it had to come. I couldn't bear
it then; can't take it now. I'll make amends.
I'm willing to agree, now. So – be fair,
there's no need to split up. We'll just be friends.
Like you suggested. Not see quite so much
of each other. Please! I agree. You're right.
I made too much of what we had. Been such
a fool. I'll take the blame. We'll start tonight
– The New Improved Regime. We'll both be free
to do just as we want – the adult way.
I'll do just as you want me to. You'll see.
I'm willing to do anything you say.
I promise. I won't make a scene. Won't cry.
If you'll do just one thing. Don't say goodbye.

MICK GOWAR

a A relationship between two people who were deeply in love is 'going wrong'. Look closely at all the evidence in the poem and explain why.

b What is the woman most concerned about? What are the man's chief concerns? Are their concerns the same?

c In your opinion, are the feelings expressed by 'She' more typical of women than of men, and are the feelings expressed by 'He' more typical of men than of women?

d She says, 'we're still happy' and 'we still get along'. He says, 'there's no need to split up' and 'we'll start tonight – The New Improved Regime'. In your opinion, what chance is there of their relationship reviving and surviving? Refer to the text to support your views.

e Do you think the form and style of this poem is effective? Give reasons. Why might Mick Gowar have chosen to set it out in the way he does?

The poem   Read the poem below to yourself, twice. On the second reading, pay particular attention to the comparisons used in the first stanza.

A Birthday

My heart is like a singing bird
  Whose nest is in a watered shoot;
My heart is like an apple tree
  Whose boughs are bent with thickset fruit;
My heart is like a rainbow shell
  That paddles in a **halcyon** sea;
My heart is gladder than all these
  Because my love is come to me.

Raise me a **dais** of silk and **down**;
  Hang it with **vair** and purple dyes;
Carve it in doves and pomegranates,
  And peacocks with a hundred eyes;
Work it in gold and silver grapes,
  In leaves and silver **fleur-de-lys**;
Because the birthday of my life
  Is come, my love is come to me.

CHRISTINA ROSSETTI

halcyon: calm and peaceful
dais: a platform used for important ceremonial occasions
down: soft feathers
vair: rich fur, used as a decorative trimming
fleur-de-lys: literally, 'the flower of the lily', the former royal emblem of France

Post-reading activities on 'A Birthday'

ACTIVITY 2   *Similes and similarities (1)*

The poem's first stanza is composed mostly of similes: 'My heart is like . . .'

In a small group, consider what Christina Rossetti tells us about her feelings by making an analysis of the three similes she uses to describe them. Copy the following table into your book or file and fill in your conclusions.

	The lover's heart is like . . .		
	a singing bird	*an apple tree*	*a seashell*
What ideas does this simile suggest about being in love?			
How well does this simile match up with the other two?			
How effectively does this simile describe the feeling of being deeply in love?			

As a class, compare the conclusions you have reached with those of other groups and with those of your teacher.

ACTIVITY 3   *Queen of Hearts*

In the poem's second stanza, Christina Rossetti imagines herself as a queen, possibly at her coronation ceremony. (Many of the references are to medieval heraldry.)

As a class, imagine the ceremony described in stanza 2 as being equivalent to a modern wedding. Many 'trappings' of a wedding are not just decorative but are also intended to be symbolic, for example, the bride's white dress and silver horseshoes. What others come to mind?

Consider the trappings of Christina Rossetti's 'ceremony'. In your opinion, do they simply create a vague impression of someone feeling special because she is joyfully in love, or do they have a more particular symbolic meaning and importance?

ACTIVITY 4   *An expression of love*

This poem was, and still is, one of the most popular love poems in English Literature. In a small group, give an honest opinion about how effective you find it as an expression of the happiness that being in love can bring.

The poem Read the poem below to yourself, twice. The second time through, begin to form some impressions of the way its subject-matter is different from Christina Rossetti's.

My Heart is Like a Withered Nut

My heart is like a withered nut,
  Rattling within its hollow shell;
You cannot open my breast, and put
  Anything fresh with it to dwell.
The hopes and dreams that filled it when
  Life's spring of glory met my view,
Are gone! and ne'er with joy or pain
  That shrunken heart shall swell anew.

My heart is like a withered nut;
  Once it was soft to every touch,
But now 'tis **stern** and closely shut –
  I would not have to plead with such.
Each light-toned voice once cleared my brow,
  Each gentle breeze once shook the tree
Where hung the sun-lit fruit, which now
  Lies cold, and stiff, and sad, like me!

My heart is like a withered nut –
  It once was **comely** to the view;
But since misfortune's blast hath cut,
  It hath a dark and mournful **hue**.
The freshness of its **verdant** youth
  Nought to that fruit can now restore;
And my poor heart, I feel in truth,
  Nor sun, nor smile shall light it **more**.

CAROLINE NORTON

stern: hard
comely: attractive
hue: colour
verdant: green-coloured
Nor: neither
more: again

106

Post-reading activities on 'My Heart is Like a Withered Nut'

<u>ACTIVITY 5</u>　　　*Poetry and prose*

On your own, put yourself in Caroline Norton's place. Using the first person ('I', 'me', 'my' etc.) write three prose paragraphs, one for each stanza, summarising as clearly as possible the feelings expressed in this poem. Take as much space as you need. It is important to be both precise and detailed in what you write.

As a class, consider what Caroline Norton gains or loses by writing in the form of a poem rather than in prose sentences and paragraphs.

<u>ACTIVITY 6</u>　　　*Similes and similarities (2)*

Each stanza of the poem is based on a simile – or, more precisely, on different aspects of the same simile: 'My heart is like a withered nut'.

In a small group, consider what Caroline Norton tells us about her feelings by making an analysis of the similes she uses to describe them. Copy the following table into your book or file and fill in your conclusions.

	The lover's heart is like . . .		
	a nut in a hollow shell (stanza 1)	a nut turned hard and cold (stanza 2)	a nut turned old and ugly (stanza 3)
What ideas does this suggest about the loss of love?			
How does this aspect of the nut simile link up with those in other stanzas?			
How effectively does this simile describe the feelings of a betrayed lover?			

As a class, compare the conclusions you have reached with those of other groups and with those of your teacher.

<hr>

ACTIVITY 7   *Comparing the comparisons*

By yourself, write an analysis of 'A Birthday' and 'My Heart is Like a Withered Nut', focusing mainly on the poets' use of comparisons. Your work in Activities 2 and 6 will be of the most help to you here.

Concentrate less on explaining the comparisons than on making an honest personal judgement about how effectively the poets use them. Conclude your account by saying which poem is, in your opinion, the more successful of the two in this respect.

For further comparison

Below are two more pre-twentieth-century poems suitable for comparing with those in this unit or with each other.

How Do I Love Thee?

How do I love thee? Let me count the ways.
    I love thee to the depth and breadth and height
    My soul can reach, when feeling out of sight
For the ends of Being and ideal Grace.
I love thee to the level of every day's
    Most quiet need, by sun and candlelight.
    I love thee freely, as men strive for Right;
I love thee purely, as they turn from Praise.
I love thee with the passion put to use
    In my old griefs, and with my childhood's faith.
I love thee with a love I seemed to lose
    With my lost saints – I love thee with the breath,
Smiles, tears, of all my life! – and, if God choose,
    I shall but love thee better after death

ELIZABETH BARRETT BROWNING

Failed Lives

A year ago we walked the wood –
   A year ago today;
A blackbird fluttered round her brood
   Deep in the white-flowered may.

We trod the happy woodland ways,
   Where sunset streamed between
The hazel stems in long dusk rays,
   And turned to gold the green.

A thrush sang where the ferns uncurled;
   And clouds of wind-flowers grew:
I missed the meaning of the world
   From lack of love for you.

You missed the beauty of the year,
   And failed its self to see,
Through too much doubt and too much fear,
   And too much love of me.

This year we hear the birds' glad strain,
   Again the sunset glows,
We walk the wild wet woods again,
   Again the wind-flower blows.

In cloudy white the falling may
   Drifts down the scented wind,
And so the secret drifts away
   Which we shall never find.

Our drifted spirits are not free
   Spring's secret springs to touch,
For now you do not care for me,
   And I love you too much.

EDITH NESBIT

Home-Thoughts, From Abroad
ROBERT BROWNING

The Teacher's Monologue
CHARLOTTE BRONTË

This unit is designed with a single aim in mind: to help you prepare for writing about poetry under examination conditions. Your teacher will decide whether you should work on it entirely by yourself or with some measure of support.

Both poems are written by people who, being away from home, long to be back in familiar surroundings. Robert Browning, living in Italy, is prompted by the arrival of spring to think nostalgically about the English countryside where he grew up. Charlotte Brontë, in her first teaching post, is separated from her close-knit family less by distance than by the fact that she is living and working among strangers.

You will need your own photocopy of each poem before you begin working on this unit.

The poem   Read the poem below twice, using the photocopy. Spend about five minutes looking through it. Do not look at all at 'The Teacher's Monologue'.

On your first reading, make yourself go through the poem much more slowly than you would normally and try to 'hear' it in your head. If you lose the thread of what Browning is writing, stop and go back over it until you feel you have a reasonable understanding of the meaning.

The second time through, jot down in very brief note form the main ideas or feelings you are sure the poem contains, however obvious they may seem. For example, for another poem you might find yourself making the following notes: 'Feels afraid he may die. Thinks back to childhood. Does God care if he dies? Wonders if he'll be missed'.

Home-Thoughts, From Abroad

Oh, to be in England
Now that April's there,
And whoever wakes in England
Sees, some morning, unaware,
That the lowest boughs and the brush-wood sheaf   5
Round the elm-tree **bole** are in tiny leaf,
While the chaffinch sings on the orchard bough
In England – now!

And after April, when May follows,
And the whitethroat builds, and all the swallows –   10
Hark! where my blossomed pear-tree in the hedge
Leans to the field and scatters on the clover
Blossoms and dewdrops – at the bent-spray's edge –
That's the wise thrush; he sings each song twice over,
Lest you should think he never could recapture   15
The first fine careless rapture!
And though the fields look rough with **hoary** dew,
All will be gay when noontide wakes anew
The buttercups, the little children's **dower**,
– Far brighter than this gaudy melon-flower!   20

ROBERT BROWNING

bole: tree-trunk
Lest: in case
hoary: white-frosted
dower: gift of nature

111

The poem Read the poem below twice, using the photocopy. Spend about five minutes looking through it. For the moment, try to put 'Home-Thoughts, From Abroad' out of your mind.

Follow exactly the same advice for reading this poem as that given for 'Home-Thoughts, From Abroad'.

The Teacher's Monologue (extract)

The room is quiet, thoughts alone
  People its mute tranquillity;
The yoke put off, the long task done, –
  I am, as it is bliss to be,
Still and untroubled. Now, I see,   5
  For the first time, how soft the day
O'er waveless water, stirless tree,
  Silent and sunny, wings its way.
Now, as I watch that distant hill,
  So faint, so blue, so far removed,   10
Sweet dreams of home my heart may fill,
  That home where I am known and loved:
It lies beyond; yon **azure** brow
  Parts me from all Earth holds for me;
And, morn and eve, my yearnings flow   15
  Thitherward tending, changelessly.
My happiest hours, ay! all the time,
  I love to keep in memory,
Lapsed among moors, ere life's first prime
  Decayed to dark anxiety.   20

CHARLOTTE BRONTË

People: inhabit, fill up
The yoke put off: the burden laid aside
azure: sky-blue
Lapsed: spent in a carefree way

Post-reading activities on both poems

<u>ACTIVITY 1</u>   *The order of things*

Many poets, especially those writing before 1900, use a different word order from that of modern everyday speech. The next stage in adding to your understanding, therefore, is to check the order of words in each poem wherever the meaning seems obscure.

It helps enormously to read from 'pause to pause' rather than line by line. Also bear in mind that the grammar of a poem does not always follow the grammar pattern of a typical prose sentence: poets tend to be more free in their use of grammar, often in order to highlight certain words and phrases.

Spend at least another five minutes re-reading the following parts of each poem and deciding on your answers to the questions about each. Jot down notes if you wish.

Home-Thoughts, From Abroad

✧ 'whoever wakes in England
    Sees . . . ' (lines 3–4). What do they see?

✧ What is it that 'scatters on the clover' (line 12)?

✧ What is it that 'noontide wakes anew' (line 18)?

The Teacher's Monologue

✧ What 'people' the room in which the poet is sitting (line 2)?

✧ What 'wings its way', and to where (line 8)?

✧ What does the poet 'love to keep in memory' (line 18)?

Ask your own questions similar to those above about any other parts of the poems that you still do not fully understand.

<u>ACTIVITY 2</u>   *Comparing and contrasting (1)*

In an examination, you are frequently asked to compare and contrast certain aspects of two poems. Bear in mind that 'compare' means 'point out the ways in which they are alike', whereas 'contrast' means 'point out the ways in which they differ'.

In this case, you are asked to compare and contrast the two poets' feelings about being away from their homes.

Before beginning to write your answer, note down some key ideas. Add in line references. Do it like this:

Similarities	Line(s)		Differences	Line(s)	
	RB	CB		RB	CB
Both RB and CB feel that where they **are** is a less pleasant and happy place than where they **want to be**	7–8	13–14	RB misses the English countryside most. CB misses her home and family most	11–14	11–12

Now begin writing your answer. It is better to make one key point per paragraph than to combine several points together in the same paragraph, however closely your points may be connected. For each key point you make, you will be given credit if you can back it up with a quotation, hence the importance of line references in your notes. Examiners also expect you to be able to comment on the quotations you make, in order to show your appreciation of the poet's use of language.

Therefore, three components make up a well-planned answer:

Statement → Quotation → Comment

Two well-detailed paragraphs contrasting the poets' feelings about being away from home might be written as follows:

Browning's strongest feeling about being away from home is that, living abroad in Italy, he misses the fertile beauty of an English spring: **Statement**

> *'Hark! where my blossomed pear-tree in the hedge*
> *Leans to the field and scatters on the clover*
> *Blossoms and dewdrops . . .'* **Quotation**

This description, referring twice to 'blossom', shows that Browning associates April in England with ripeness, delicate colours and freshness, an impression strengthened by the emphasis on 'dewdrops'. In Italy, by contrast, he can see only 'this gaudy melon-flower', which suggests that its colouring is too harsh and showy to please him. **Comment**

Charlotte Brontë, on the other hand, misses the countryside less than she misses her home and family: **Statement**

'Sweet dreams of home my heart may fill,
That home where I am known and loved:
It lies beyond . . .'

} **Quotation**

Home is where her 'heart' is. Her thoughts of home are 'sweet' as she 'dreams' of being there with her family by whom she is 'known and loved'. The emphasis on 'loved' shows that she is now among people by whom she is **not** loved, thus making her home sickness all the more painful to bear.

} **Comment**

ACTIVITY 3   *Comparing and contrasting (2)*

As well as pointing out similarities and differences in the subject-matter of two poems, you will also be asked to comment on the style in which they are written.

What do examiners expect you to comment on? Below is a brief checklist, which you can use to write about any poem under exam conditions. It is deliberately set out in question form because you need to get used to asking your own questions when you are faced with this kind of task.

1   In what ways is the poet's **choice of language** appropriate to what he or she is writing about? This includes (i) single words and phrases; (ii) use of comparisons (that is, simile, metaphor and personification). See Unit 3.

2   How does the poem's **form** reflect, or match up with, its subject-matter? This includes (i) the way it is divided into stanzas; (ii) the use of particular styles such as the ballad form (Unit 6) and the sonnet (Unit 11).

3   How is the **rhythm** at any particular point in the poem suited to what is being described? See, in particular, Unit 9.

4   How does the **sound** of certain words and phrases echo the poem's meaning? See, in particular, Units 2 and 8.

5   What is the poet's dominant **tone**? How does this reflect (i) his or her feelings; (ii) his or her own attitude towards the poem's subject? See Unit 10.

6   If the poem rhymes, what purposes does the poet's **rhyme scheme** serve? If it is written in free verse or blank verse, why has the poet chosen to leave the poem unrhymed? See Units 7 and 11.

Explore your response to the style in which Browning and Charlotte Brontë write by answering the following questions. These are selective: as in examinations, it is impossible to cover everything. Answer in note form for the moment.

Home-Thoughts, From Abroad

✧ Why do you think Browning begins the poem with the exclamation 'Oh . . . '?

✧ Two words are repeated, and therefore strongly emphasised, in stanza 1: 'now' and 'England'. Why?

✧ The eight lines of stanza 1 are made up of a single sentence. There are no pauses at the end of lines 1, 3, 5 and 7. How does this serve to create a particular rhythm and tone in the first part of the poem? How does the tone help to convey Browning's feelings towards his subject?

✧ In stanza 2, Browning's descriptions depend heavily on the use of common nouns (i.e. names), to such an extent that they almost turn into a list: 'whitethroat', 'swallows', 'pear-tree', 'hedge', 'clover', 'blossom', 'thrush', 'buttercups', etc. What reasons do you think Browning has for writing in this way?

✧ To what does 'the first fine careless rapture!' (line 16) refer, and what exactly does it mean? How might it be seen to be the key line in the poem as a whole?

✧ What is the effect of the last line of the poem, linked as it is by rhyme to line 19?

The Teacher's Monologue

✧ What mood, or feeling, is evoked by the succession of alliterated words in lines 5 to 8: 'still', 'soft', 'stirless', 'silent', 'sunny'?

✧ Is this mood appropriate to the first part of Charlotte Brontë's poem?

✧ Where would you say that the mood of the poem changes? What aspects of its style indicate this change?

✧ How would you describe the rhythm of lines 15 and 16? In what ways is this rhythm suited to expressing Charlotte Brontë's feelings at this stage of the poem?

✧ In the poem's last line, how and why is such a strong emphasis given to the words 'decayed' and 'dark'?

ACTIVITY 4   *Commenting on style*

Now draw on your notes from Activity 3 to write a detailed account of the way in which the style of each poem reflects its meaning. Make some comparisons between the two poets' choices of language and of form to express their feelings about being 'exiled' from home.

For further comparison

The pre-twentieth-century poem below is suitable for comparing with either of the poems in this unit.

'Tis Strange To Me . . .

'Tis strange to me, who long have seen no face
That was not like a book whose every page
I knew by heart, a kindly common-place –
And faithful record of progressive age –
To wander forth and view an unknown race;
Of all that I have been to find no trace,
No footstep of my by-gone pilgrimage.
Thousands I pass, and no one stays his pace
To tell me that the day is fair, or rainy –
Each one his object seeks with anxious chase,
And I have not a common hope with any –
Thus like one drop of oil upon a flood,
In uncommunicating solitude –
Single am I amongst the countless many.

HARTLEY COLERIDGE

14

Fallen to dust

Remembrance   EMILY BRONTË

Requiescat   OSCAR WILDE

In this unit, both poems are about the death of a loved one.
Emily Brontë expresses her feelings of grief for 'my only Love',
fifteen years after his death. Oscar Wilde's poem is a memorial
for the death of his 13 year-old sister, written shortly after the
event.

The poem   Read the following poem twice, first on your own and then with a partner. The second time through, read the eight stanzas aloud, turn by turn.

Remembrance

Cold in the earth – and the deep snow piled above thee,
   Far, far **removed**, cold in the dreary grave!
Have I forgot, my only Love, to love thee,
   Severed at last by Time's all-severing wave?

Now, when alone, do my thoughts no longer hover
   Over the mountains, on **that northern shore**,
Resting their wings where heath and fern-leaves cover
   Thy noble heart for ever, ever more?

Cold in the earth – and **fifteen wild Decembers**
   From those brown hills, have melted into spring:
Faithful, indeed, is the spirit that remembers
   After such years of change and suffering!

Sweet Love of youth, forgive, if I forget thee,
   While the world's tide is bearing me along;
Other desires and other hopes beset me,
   Hopes which obscure, but cannot do thee wrong!

No later light has lightened up my heaven,
   No second morn has ever shone for me;
All my life's bliss from thy dear life was given,
   All my life's bliss is in the grave with thee.

But when the days of golden dreams had perished,
   And even Despair was powerless to destroy,
Then did I learn how existence could be cherished,
   Strengthened, and fed, without the aid of joy.

Then did I check the tears of useless passion
   Weaned my young soul from yearning after thine;
Sternly denied its burning wish to hasten
   Down to that tomb already more than mine.

And, even yet, I dare not let it **languish**,
    Dare not indulge in memory's rapturous pain;
Once drinking deep of that divinest anguish,
    How could I seek the empty world again?

E<small>MILY</small> B<small>RONTË</small>

removed: distant
that northern shore: where her lover is buried
fifteen wild Decembers: fifteen winters have passed since he died
languish: lapse into misery

Post-reading activities on 'Remembrance'

___

A<small>CTIVITY</small> 1   *Charting the poet's feelings*

With a partner, draw a large circle and divide it into eight numbered segments.
Each segment represents one stanza of the poem.

Talk about the main feelings that Emily Brontë expresses in each stanza. Then,
in your own words and in only one sentence, write in each segment a summary
of the poet's feelings stanza by stanza. Do it like this:

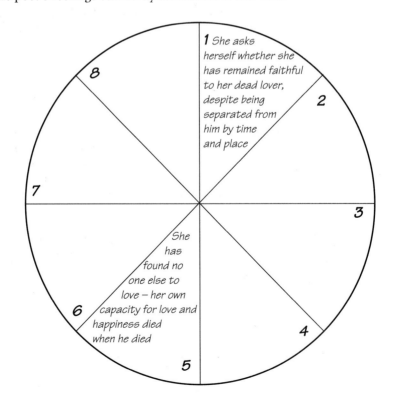

By yourself, use your summary notes to write, in your own words, a full account of the poet's feelings as she remembers her lover's death. Quote from the text to illustrate every feeling you describe.

ACTIVITY 2   *Subject-matter and style*

In a small group or as a class, look closely at the way in which each stanza of 'Remembrance' is written. Consider the questions below to judge how well-suited Emily Brontë's style of writing is to conveying her feelings.

Stanza 1

✧ Our first impression of the dead lover is that he is 'cold' in his grave, covered by 'deep snow', and 'far, far removed'. Does this mean that Emily Brontë's feelings for him have become cold?

✧ How does the sound and rhythm of lines 1 and 2 reflect their meaning?

✧ What metaphor does Emily Brontë use in line 4? Do you find it effective in the context of the whole stanza?

Stanza 2

✧ With what does Emily Brontë compare her thoughts about her dead lover in this stanza? Why?

✧ What is the effect of the repetition in 'for ever, ever more'?

Stanza 3

✧ What impressions are we given of the length of time that has passed since her lover's death by the poet's choice of the words 'wild' and 'melted'?

✧ Whose spirit has been 'faithful'? How is the idea of faithfulness given emphasis by the style of the last two lines in this stanza?

Stanza 4

✧ What metaphor does Emily Brontë use in the second line? How does it link up with the metaphor used in the first stanza?

✧ The last line is divided by a comma into two equal parts. How does this 'middle stop', or *caesura*, reinforce the meaning of the line?

Stanza 5

✧ With what is the dead lover metaphorically compared in lines 1 and 2? What do these comparisons show about the poet's feelings for him, both at the time and after he died?

✧ What effect is achieved by the repetitions at the start of lines 1 and 2 and at the start of lines 3 and 4?

Stanza 6

✧ Why does Emily Brontë describe the time she spent with her lover as 'the days of golden dreams'? At what stage do you think these days might have 'perished'?

✧ What is the effect of personifying 'despair' in line 2? Can you see any purpose in the poet's alliteration of 'despair' and 'destroy'?

Stanza 7

✧ Comment on the choice and meaning of the verbs 'check', 'weaned', 'denied' and 'hasten'. How strong do you judge the poet's wish to die with her lover to have been?

✧ Why does Emily Brontë see her lover's tomb as being 'already more than mine'?

Stanza 8

✧ What is the meaning of 'memory's rapturous pain'? How can pain be thought of as 'rapturous'?

✧ What is the meaning of 'divinest anguish'? How might anguish be felt to be 'divine'?

✧ Do you think that Emily Brontë's feelings in this last stanza are confused and uncertain, or are they clear and decisive?

The poem as a whole

✧ How would you describe the dominant tone of the poem?

✧ Emily Brontë writes as if she is speaking to, rather than about, her dead lover. What effects does she gain by doing so?

✧ 'Remembrance' has been described as 'a sentimental wallowing in grief which is embarrassingly self-indulgent'. Do you think there is any truth in this criticism?

The poem   Read the following poem twice to yourself. Then read it aloud to a partner, using a suitable tone and volume.

Requiescat

Tread lightly, she is near
　　Under the snow,
Speak gently, she can hear
　　The daises grow.

All her bright golden hair
　　Tarnished with rust,
She that was young and fair
　　Fallen to dust.

Lily-like, white as snow,
　　She hardly knew
She was a woman, so
　　Sweetly she grew.

Coffin-board, heavy stone,
　　Lie on her breast;
I vex my heart alone,
　　She is at rest.

Peace, peace; she cannot hear
　　Lyre or sonnet;
All my life's buried here.
　　Heap earth upon it.

OSCAR WILDE

Requiescat: Rest in peace
Tarnished: stained, blemished
Lyre: an ancient harp, often played to accompany a mournful song – the lyre-flower is also called 'bleeding heart'

Post-reading activities on 'Requiescat'

ACTIVITY 3	*'She is at rest'*

In a small group, discuss, and make your own notes on, all the ways in which Oscar Wilde evokes a feeling of peacefulness and tranquillity in this poem. Consider not only his choice of words and images, but also:

✧ the sound of words.

✧ the rhythm of the lines.

✧ the tone of the poem as a whole.

As a class, discuss what impressions of his dead sister Wilde gives in 'Requiescat'. What are his own feelings about her death?

ACTIVITY 4	*In comparison*

The two poems in this unit are **elegies** – that is, poems written in the form of a lament for the dead.

On your own, write a detailed comparison between the elegies 'Remembrance' and 'Requiescat', paying attention to the following.

✧ Compare and contrast the feelings towards the dead person expressed by each poet.

✧ 'Emily Brontë evokes a sense of passion; Oscar Wilde conveys a mood of peace.' Consider the subject-matter and style of each poem in order to assess the truth of this statement.

✧ '"Requiescat" is a lament for a dead sister; "Remembrance" is less of a lament for Emily Brontë's dead lover than a lament for herself.' Say, with reasons, how far you agree with this comment.

✧ Bearing in mind all the work you have done in this unit, say which poem you find more effective as an elegy.

Throughout your commentary, use quotations from the poems to illustrate your ideas and to support your arguments.

For further comparison

The nineteenth-century poem below is suitable for comparison with either of the poems in this unit.

There's Been a Death

There's been a death in the opposite house
As lately as today.
I know it by the numb look
Such houses have alway.

The neighbours rustle in and out,
The doctor drives away.
A window opens like a pod,
Abrupt, mechanically;

Somebody flings a mattress out.
The children hurry by;
They wonder if it died on that.
I used to, when **a boy**.

The minister goes stiffly in
As if the house were his
And he owned all the mourners now,
And little boys besides;

And then the milliner, and the man
Of the appalling trade
To take the measure of the house.
There'll be that dark parade

Of tassels and of coaches soon.
It's easy as a sign –
The intuition of the news
In just a country town.

EMILY DICKINSON

a boy: Emily Dickinson sometimes used a male 'persona' in her writing

The Old Familiar Faces
CHARLES LAMB

Tears, Idle Tears
ALFRED, LORD TENNYSON

This final unit is intended to be used as a revision unit for GCSE/Standard Grade exams. It will be helpful, but not essential, to have already worked through Unit 13 with its detailed advice on how to write about poetry under exam conditions.

Charles Lamb and Alfred, Lord Tennyson both look back to an earlier part of their lives and express one principle emotion: regret for 'the days that are no more'. They are saddened by the changes that the passing of time has brought about.

You can regard this unit as pure exam practice, in which case you need only look at pages 127–8. Alternatively, if you feel less confident, follow the guidance given on pages 129–31.

The Old Familiar Faces

Where are they gone, the old familiar faces?

I had a mother, but she died, and left me,
Died prematurely in a day of horrors –
All, all are gone, the old familiar faces.

I have had playmates, I have had companions,   5
In my days of childhood, in my joyful school-days –
All, all are gone, the old familiar faces.

I have been laughing, I have been **carousing**,
Drinking late, sitting late, with my **bosom cronies** –
All, all are gone, the old familiar faces.   10

I loved a love once, fairest among women.
Closed are her doors to me, I must not see her –
All, all are gone, the old familiar faces.

I have a friend, a kinder friend has no man.
Like an **ingrate**, I left my friend abruptly;   15
Left him, to muse on the old familiar faces.

Ghost-like, I paced round the haunts of my childhood.
Earth seem'd a desert I was bound to **traverse**,
Seeking to find the old familiar faces.

Friend of my bosom, thou more than a brother!   20
Why wert thou not born in my father's dwelling?
So might we talk of the old familiar faces.

For some they have died, and some they have left me,
And some are taken from me; all are departed;
All, all are gone, the old familiar faces.   25

CHARLES LAMB

carousing: making merry
bosom cronies: closest friends
ingrate: an ungrateful and selfish person
traverse: travel across

Tears, Idle Tears

Tears, **idle** tears, I know not what they mean,
Tears from the depth of some divine despair
Rise in the heart, and gather to the eyes,
In looking on the happy Autumn-fields,
And thinking of the days that are no more.   5

Fresh as the first beam glittering on a sail,
That brings our friends up from the underworld,
Sad as **the last** which reddens over one
That sinks with all we love below the **verge**;
So sad, so fresh, the days that are no more.   10

Ah, sad and strange as in dark summer dawns
The earliest pipe of half-awaken'd birds
To dying ears, when unto dying eyes
The **casement** slowly grows a glimmering square;
So sad, so strange, the days that are no more.   15

Dear as remember'd kisses after death,
And sweet as those by hopeless **fancy feign'd**
On lips that are for others; deep as love,
Deep as first love, and wild with all regret;
O Death in Life, the days that are no more.   20

ALFRED, LORD TENNYSON

idle: foolish, worthless
the last: i.e. the last beam of the sun
verge: horizon
casement: window
fancy: imagination
feign'd: pretended, made up

Exam question

Write a detailed comparison between 'The Old Familiar Faces' and 'Tears, Idle Tears'. You should consider in the course of your comments:

✦ each poet's feelings about the past.

✦ the way in which these feelings are expressed.

✦ which poem, in your opinion, conveys its theme more effectively.

Guidance for planning and writing your comparison

<u>PART 1</u>   *First impressions*

After reading each poem twice, note down your immediate responses to the questions which follow.

Subject-matter

The Old Familiar Faces

◇ How many things cause Lamb to feel sad? What do they have in common?

◇ What evidence is there that Lamb feels deeply about what he has lost?

◇ Is there one phrase more than any other which Lamb uses to sum up his feelings of loss?

Tears, Idle Tears

◇ What causes Tennyson to weep? Does he feel sad for the same reasons as Lamb does?

◇ Compared with Lamb, how deeply do you think Tennyson feels about what he has lost?

◇ Is there one phrase more than any other which Tennyson uses to sum up his feelings of loss?

Style

The Old Familiar Faces

◇ Apart from the first line which stands by itself, Lamb's poem consists of eight stanzas. For what reason might he have chosen to divide up his poem like this?

◇ Most of the stanzas begin and end in a similar way, with a *refrain* (that is, a repeated phrase). What effect do you think Lamb is aiming for by the use of this device?

◇ How would you describe the dominant tone of the poem?

Tears, Idle Tears

◇ Tennyson's poem consists of four stanzas. For what reason might he have chosen to divide up his poem like this?

◇ Like Lamb's poem, each stanza ends with a refrain. What effect do you think Tennyson is aiming for by the use of this device?

◇ How would you describe the dominant tone of the poem?

129

<hr>
PART 2   *Developing your ideas*

You should now have a reasonably clear idea of what the poems are about and of the similarities between them. Take your first response further by answering the questions which follow.

Subect-matter

The Old Familiar Faces

✧ Lamb writes 'All, all are gone'. Does he mean that all the people he loved are dead, or have some of them 'gone' for other reasons?

✧ Which of the losses that Lamb has suffered do you think have caused him most sadness? What evidence can you find for your answer?

✧ What impressions does Lamb give of the present compared with the past?

Tears, Idle Tears

✧ Why do you think it is the sight of 'Autumn-fields' that triggers off Tennyson's thoughts about the past?

✧ For what reason are Tennyson's memories of 'the days that are no more' like 'Death in Life'?

Style

The Old Familiar Faces

✧ Look at lines 17 and 18. Why do you think Lamb compares himself to a ghost? Why do you think he compares earth to a desert?

✧ Throughout the poem, how much use does Lamb make of repetition as a stylistic device? Find several examples. Do you find these effective?

✧ How fully would you say the last stanza summarises what Lamb has written earlier in the poem?

Tears, Idle Tears

✧ The key words in stanza 2 to describe 'the days that are no more' are 'fresh' and 'sad'. Tennyson illustrates this idea by using a simile. What is it? Do you find it effective?

✧ The key words in stanza 3 to describe 'the days that are no more' are 'sad' and 'strange'. Tennyson illustrates this idea by using another simile. What is it? Do you find it effective?

✧ The key words in stanza 4 to describe 'the days that are no more' are 'dear' and 'sweet'. Tennyson illustrates this idea by using several connected similes. What are they? Do you find them effective?

PART 3   *Shaping your answer*

You are now in a position to write your answer to the question on page 128. Note that it asks you to write a detailed comparison between the two poems.

This means that you should *not* make all your comments on 'The Old Familiar Faces' in the first part of your answer, followed by all your comments on 'Tears, Idle Tears' in the second half. Far more credit will be earned by making one major point about Lamb's poem, then following it with a comparative point about Tennyson's poem. An example of how your answer should be organised is given in Unit 13 (see page 114–5).

As you make each major point in your answer, try to illustrate it with suitable quotations from the two poems.

Now draw on the ideas you have formed about 'The Old Familiar Faces' and 'Tears, Idle Tears' to write your answer as if you were working under exam conditions. Write a total of six paragraphs, using each of the points below to build up one paragraph.

Paragraph prompts

1   What makes each poet sad? Do Lamb and Tennyson feel sad about the same things?

2   How does each poet show that he feels devastated when he thinks back to what he has lost?

3   Each poet makes a strong contrast between the past and the present. How does he bring out this contrast?

4   Why do Lamb and Tennyson divide up their poems into eight and four stanzas respectively?

5   Both poets use repetition and a refrain in constructing their stanzas. What effects do they achieve in doing so?

6   Lamb expresses his feelings mainly through making direct statements; Tennyson expresses his feelings mainly through the use of similes. Which technique do you find more effective, and why?

Index of first lines